The
CRABCHURCH
CONSPIRACY
1645

The Trve Story of
Dorset's Bloodiest Secret

Mark Vine

Foreword by Professor Ronald Hutton

The Crabchurch Conspiracy 1645

Copyright © 2013 Mark Vine. All rights reserved.
First paperback edition printed 2013 in the United Kingdom.

A catalogue record for this book is available from the British
Library.
ISBN 978-0-9927835-0-1

Published by Mark Vine.

For more copies of this book, please visit:
www.crabchurch.co.uk or
www.thedolmen.com

Printed by Sherrens Printing Ltd. Weymouth
www.sherrens.com

Printed in Great Britain.

This book is dedicated to the memory of my very dear and much missed
friend 'The Great Steve Baker' and to his three beautiful girls,
Marina, Sukie and Rosie.

Commanding Officer,
Colonel William Sydenham's
Regiment of Foote,
English Civil War Society
1980-97... and forever more.

Contents

Map of Weymouth and Melcombe During the Seventeenth Century

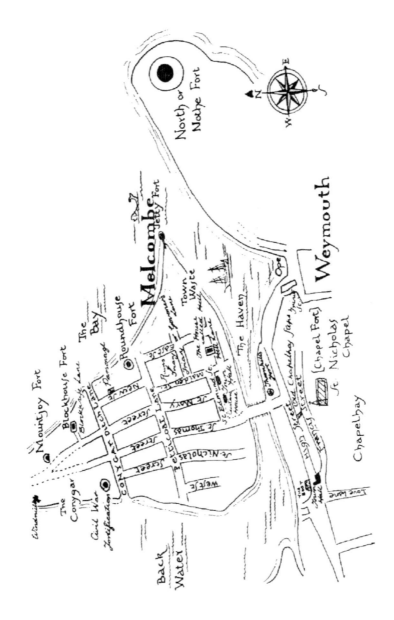

Map of Dorset

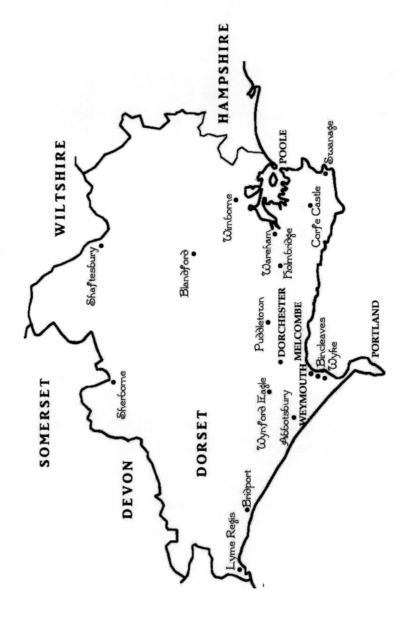

Foreword

By Professor Ronald Hutton

Professor of History at University of Bristol
MA(Cantab), DPhil(Oxon), FRHistS, FSA
Fellow of the Royal Historical Society
Fellow of the Society of Antiquaries

The civil wars of the 1640s were probably the worst experience that the people of the British Isles have ever undergone. Epidemics of disease killed far greater numbers of human beings in a shorter time than these conflicts ever did, but left people's sense of their world, their religious, political and social beliefs and their relations with each other, more or less intact. The civil strife destroyed all of those things. England went through three civil wars between 1642 and 1651, of which the first and biggest, which ended in 1646, killed about 100,000 people outright in a population of just five million, and left about another 150,000 to die by inches of wounds, while in battle-torn areas civilian burials rose far over the average as illness, hunger and poverty all increased amid local economies wrecked by the fighting. Trade was disrupted all over the nation, and crushing war taxation ground down incomes further, so that even communities which never heard a shot fired in anger went into deep economic recession. Those in war zones had houses and crops burned, and livestock slaughtered or stolen. Perhaps a quarter of the entire adult male population of England served as soldiers at some point in the Great Civil War, a degree of militarisation never experienced before or since, just as the loss of life was the greatest ever known as a percentage of the people, dwarfing that in the World Wars. This was no war between states, as in America in the 1860s, because across the nation virtually every district was divided between rival partisans, and the fault lines of ideological hatred ran through villages, households and families. This really was a conflict in which fathers fought sons, brothers against brother, and mothers and children disowned each other. The ideas for which they contended amounted to different visions of how the Church, the political system and the social order should be, and in an important sense England has never recovered from the clash. Ever since, what was formerly a largely united and consensual nation has been divided between two political parties representing different senses of what it means to be English, and a Church which had commanded the loyalty of all but five per cent of the population has been shattered into large numbers of nonconformist Protestant denominations, such as Presbyterians, Congregationalists, Baptists and Quakers. Ever since then, also, Parliament has been an essential and almost constant component of political life, providing an arena in which differences of opinion can constantly be expressed. The effect on Scotland and Ireland was proportionately more dramatic. The loss of life in the civil wars there was even worse (a fifth to a third of all the Irish dying), and it left the self-confidence of Scotland shattered, leading subsequently to a union with England which is only now unravelling, while a Protestant Ascendancy was imposed on Ireland which endured until 1922 and remains in a bitterly divided north of the island.

The Civil War therefore deeply matters, and part of the excitement of learning about it derives from the fact that it was at once a national conflict and a patchwork of local struggles. As such, it combines the interest of the grand epic and the kitchen-sink drama. As a county, Dorset shared, and suffered, to the full in both aspects. It had the unhappy characteristic of being one of those areas which were contested between the two parties, lying in a frontier zone between their core territories. It also has another grim feature, of being involved in action throughout the war, from the siege of Sherborne Castle in 1642 to those of Corfe and Portland Castles in 1646. It was never granted a moment of reprieve from the violence, and its rich farmlands and its ports, so strategically sited for the overseas trade to which both sides looked for income and military supplies, made each part of it a rich prize. Such was the fate of the circle of communities centred on Weymouth, the only port which the royalists managed to capture and hold for a significant length of time. They passed from the hands of one party to another in a succession of episodes of violence. Each was divided internally, between royalists and parliamentarians. For a time in 1645 the twin towns of Weymouth and Melcombe were in different hands, and Weymouth became a battlefield, and even when they were reunited in the cause of Parliament, Portland held out for the king, into another year. The struggle for Dorset threw some of the personalities who engaged in it into high relief, making them national heroes and villains, such as Sir Lewis Dyve, the diehard royalist commander, William Sydenham, who became one of Oliver Cromwell's Council of State as Lord Protector, and Anthony Ashley Cooper, the savage and supple schemer who, after various changes of side, grew into one of the leading politicians of the later seventeenth century.

Mark Vine's new edition of his already well-loved book, "The Crabchurch Conspiracy", is the best work ever written about the dramatic events in and around Weymouth during the war, and the rise to prominence of the Sydenham family which they produced. It is built on the greatest depth of research yet carried out into them, including texts in which the people who shared in those upheavals speak vividly of the hopes, hatreds, horrors and raptures which they experienced. Mark clearly has his own favourite characters, but throughout does justice to all involved, from the leaders of events to nameless soldiers who emerged from the struggle as victors or found an unmarked grave in the hillsides and fields around the town or were lost forever choking in the waters of its harbour. This is a work which brings properly to life the most dramatic and horrific sequence of experiences which this town has ever known, and which put it, at moments, at the heart of England's destiny.

***

Introduction

So much has been written about that dark period of this Island's history, commonly referred to as The 'English' Civil War that it is not my intention to add still further to the seething cauldron of debate on the causes and conclusions of it all. My wish is to simply tell a story, a true story, of what happened in the County of Dorset over three hundred and seventy years ago at the time of this country's most desperate period.

Of how a cast of many characters conspired to play their part in an enthralling saga, which culminated in three desperate weeks of intrigue, drama and blood-letting in and around what is now the bustling seaside town of Weymouth, but was then, the small, though strategically important twin towns of Weymouth and Melcombe.

It is told mainly through the eyes of one incredible family, the Sydenhams of Wynford Eagle, whose exploits in that distant and turbulent century have, for too long now, been forgotten by their fellow Dorset folk. The aim of this book is to rekindle that memory, that legend and to once again give it pride of place at the top table of Dorset's proud history.

Their heroism, guile, intelligence and sacrifice rival any of the County's heroes of the past. They are as deserving of recognition, in their own way, as any of those other great Dorset men, the maritime and literary Hardys, William Barnes, and the Tolpuddle Martyrs.

Along the way a few figures of national importance, characters that history and memory have treated more kindly, add their weight to the tapestry of events that lead up to the deadly final act played out in the streets of old Weymouth one dark, cold February night all those years ago. But the 'meat of the bones' of this tale is provided by the everyday inhabitants of Dorset, rich and poor alike, who chose their sides and risked all for the cause in which they believed, many paying the ultimate price for their choice.

To them, be they Royalist of Parliamentarian, Lord or lackey, I give my thanks, for making my mundane life shine again in the uncovering of their tale, a story of courage, fortitude and revenge.

In this book, you will be able to trace, with the aid of contemporary accounts and modern photographs, exactly where the action took place in Weymouth and other locations. You will be able to see the evidence and, with a little imagination, even hear the dead speak.

Read on, for it is here … and it is written in blood.

1

The Storm Before The Lull

In December 1641, less than a year before the start of the first English Civil War, a Dutch cargo ship called the Golden Grape left the port city of Amsterdam half laden with goods and sailed to the English port of Dover. Once there she took on more goods and an English Captain took command of her. From Dover they were bound for the big Spanish port of Cadiz and, once there, took on jars of oil, barrels of raisins and various types of wine. From there, the plan was to sail on to the port of Sanlucar de Barremeda where their voyage was to take on a somewhat more illicit air. This town was renowned for being a bullion port, a place where gold and silver plundered by the Spanish from the Americas was exchanged for all manner of goods to enable Spanish merchants to supply their colonies in the New World. In Sanlucar de Barremeda this could be done without going through the offices of officials in large ports such as Seville and a tidy profit was made all round.

In Sanlucar de Barremeda the Golden Grape's original cargo consisting of barrels of spice and pepper were exchanged for wool, silk, gold and silver coinage along with bars of silver bullion and silver plate. This exchange made the Golden Grape a very profitable vessel indeed, a veritable treasure ship.

Upon leaving Sanlucar de Barremeda, she intended to make her way up the English Channel once more to Dover, with a short, but hopefully lucrative stop over in France to trade some more. But here fate was to take a hand and play a cruel trick upon the crew and investors alike. Within sailing distance of her next goal, the intrepid little vessel was caught in a fierce channel storm and eventually she succumbed to the battering and was wrecked upon the Chesil Beach in Dorset near to the little fishing village of Wyck (Wyke Regis).

This unfortunate turn of events, although an obvious disaster for her crew, some of whom perished in the storm, was an absolute godsend for the hundreds of ordinary poor folk living along that part of the Dorset coast and for four days, much of the stricken vessel's cargo was 'salvaged' by those organised enough to take advantage of her plight.

Foremost amongst the salvagers, was a reasonably well off merchant and ship owner from Melcombe Regis called Fabian Hodder and he directed men from that town and from its neighbour, Weymouth in the process of securing as much of the cargo as they could.

Fabian Hodder was quite an extraordinary individual, a man with his fingers in many pies, a 17th century entrepreneur who would enthusiastically apply himself to any opportunity that came his way if he could see a profit in it. He was well used to managing men, and women for that matter, a skill that he was to employ to devastating and deadly effect three years after the wrecking of the Golden Grape in what became Dorset's biggest and bloodiest historical episode, known these days as The Crabchurch Conspiracy.[1] Largely forgotten for more than three hundred years, it is now becoming recognised for the important event that it undoubtedly was, not just locally, but also in the wider picture of the English Civil Wars.

---

[1] The full and fascinating story of the wrecking of the Golden Grape can be read in the author, Selwyn Williams's excellent book entitled 'Treasure of the Golden Grape' (Deadman's Bay Publishing) Selwyn Williams actually discovered and dived the wreck, bringing up many of the remaining treasures lost when she sank and all wonderfully catalogued in this great read (Williams 2012)

2

The Lull Before The Storm

As the year 1645 dawned and Britain braced itself for what was to be yet
another year of tragic Civil War, few in the Parliamentary held twin towns of
Weymouth and Melcombe had any idea of the momentous events that were
about to overwhelm them, and of the complicated plot that was to be the
catalyst for this impending catastrophe.

The two towns, divided by only a few yards of seawater had, down the years,
quarreled each with the other on many occasions, in a way that only close,
geographically intimate neighbours could. But in almost two and a half years
of the first of these civil wars, both communities had thus far escaped the
really serious death and destruction that had befallen other, less fortunate
populations.

England was being shaken to its core. Its beliefs, its traditions and indeed its
very structure would never quite be the same again. Its body-politic was
being torn apart as it had never been before and people looked on with a
mixture of both horror and indeed, on the Parliamentary side at least, some
hope that things would eventually change for the better.

Both sides in the struggle had at different times held tenure of the ports,
firstly the Parliamentarians or 'Roundheads', then the King's men, the
'Cavaliers'. Now though, at the beginning of 1645, it was the Parliamentary
faction who once more held sway there.

They had wrestled back control in June 1644 after representatives of the two
towns had ridden out to meet with the Roundhead General, Robert
Devereux, The Earl of Essex. His huge army of over six thousand men had
just swept in to the County of Dorset and was encamped only a few miles to
the east at Puddletown. The representatives' aim was to try and agree terms
of surrender for the towns and in doing so, spare the people the deadly
upheaval of a bloody siege.

A comparatively small Royalist garrison of four hundred men held the two
ports, but would probably capitulate without firing a shot against such
overwhelming odds. All ports were strategically vital in any conflict and

Weymouth and Melcombe were certainly no exception, being described by the King, Charles 1 as the "key to the kingdom".

Quite often, in this sometimes disarmingly civil Civil War, such arrangements were made and the said Royalist garrison duly left the towns a few days later without firing a shot in anger. Their officers were even permitted the courtesy of retaining their swords; the common soldiery however, was made to march out carrying only staves (A kind of cudgel). Much bloodshed on both sides now avoided, the triumphant Parliamentarians re-entered the two ports, and the nervous citizens could now only hope and pray that their efforts to parley would be honoured, as dire consequences might result if a Commander could or would not restrain his troops upon entering a surrendering community.

Dorchester had found this out to its cost on the 2nd of August 1643, when part of a Royalist army under the overall command of the Earl of Caernarvon ran riot there. This outrage was not really the fault of the Earl however, who was a man of honour. The perpetrators were troops under the command of the King's headstrong nephew, Prince Maurice, younger brother of the more famous Prince Rupert of the Rhine. The said soldiers embarked upon a sickening orgy of rape, murder and robbery and the Earl, his honour besmirched, immediately resigned his command in protest and left to join the King at the siege of Gloucester.

One can imagine then the relief in Weymouth and Melcombe when no such fate befell them on this occasion at the hands of the Parliamentarians, who re-appointed the former Governor, the formidable William Sydenham, the twenty eight year old eldest son of a local Dorset landowner.

Sydenham felt that he had been tricked out of possession of the towns the year before when, in a gesture of goodwill towards a peace initiative being organised by a certain Royalist Dorset nobleman, he was ordered by Parliament, against his better judgment, to open the gates of the towns only to be over-run by Prince Maurice's men almost immediately. Sydenham would have to wait more than a year for revenge upon the nobleman whom he saw as the architect of his loss of command, but when it came, it would be very sweet indeed as we shall discover later in this story.

3

The Fighting Sydenhams

William Sydenham was the son of a Squire and a born and bred Dorset man. His family farmed a sizeable estate at Wynford Eagle, a few miles north-west of Dorchester. The manor house where they lived still exists today. It was crowned, then as now, with a large stone eagle set high on a gable above the main door, staring out, sentinel like, from its lofty perch across the green hills towards the impressive Celtic hill-fort of Eggardon, though the present eagle is a replacement. The old one was found in the 1980s by the present owners, discarded in the old overgrown walled garden attached to the side of this magnificent building.

Wynford Eagle Manor, Home of the Sydenhams.

Sydenham's father, also named William, had for some time been a prisoner in the Royalist-held Exeter, no doubt because of his family's 'rebel stand'. But this fact had only served to strengthen the zeal of his kith and kin and now, his eldest son once more held the power of life and death over the inhabitants of Weymouth and Melcombe. There were four other sons and three sisters in this dissenting brood and the second son, Francis, with whom much of this tale is also concerned, had already gained an enviable reputation as an officer by 1645, seeming to posses the 'Midas touch' where his soldierly exploits were concerned. He appears to be the only Sydenham brother who did not attend Oxford University. After being a pupil at Dorchester Grammar School, the young man seems to have opted for a life of 'fun, games and adventure rather than scholastic achievement, though it is very plain that he did not lack intelligence when it mattered.

They were not afflicted with the dilemma facing many noble families during the civil wars, that of having close relations on opposing sides in the struggle. Indeed, with both William and Francis having gained some military experience before the war whilst serving as officers in the Dorset Trained Bands, the family were thus well placed to be a major force in the County for their chosen side.

The trained bands were local units in each English County, primarily maintained for the sole purpose of defending the population against invasion from across the water, or from the Scots to the north. At the beginning of the hostilities they were the nearest thing that either side had to a trained soldiery, apart from the much sought after mercenaries, professional soldiers who had honed their skills in the continental wars. Their services were very much in demand and handsomely rewarded.

William Sydenham was commissioned as a Captain of Horse in the army of Parliament in April 1643 and his first notable military action occurred later that year at the initial siege of Corfe Castle, set amidst the wild and beautiful Purbeck Hills of East Dorset. The castle was held by the staunchly Royalist Lady Bankes whose husband was away fighting for his King and who had left the defence of his family seat in the best and most able hands he knew.

The besieging Roundhead force was commanded by the less than adept Sir Walter Erle, who, by his own admission, was not "cut out to be a soldier". He had no success at all in trying to dislodge the much smaller, but very determined, garrison inside Corfe.

Eventually Erle, or 'Old Sir Watt' as he was known by his long-suffering men, was sent more than a hundred sailors from Poole to help with the siege. He decided in his wisdom that the best course of action would be to get the rough and ready seamen completely drunk in order to encourage them to charge up the hugely daunting hill that the castle stood upon. Alas this ploy also failed and they were easily repulsed by the defenders.

Finally, as so often happened, a much larger relieving force approached the castle, in this instance the same one that would be responsible for the sacking of Dorchester, Weymouth and Melcombe later that year, led by the King's nephew, Prince Maurice.

Apparently, upon spying the approaching Cavalier force, 'Old Sir Watt' made good his escape with such indecent haste that Royalist propagandists had a 'field day'. They maintained that when their men arrived in Corfe village, they found Erle's supper just as he had left it, laid out and uneaten upon a gravestone which he was supposedly using as a table and that furthermore, the food was still piping hot!

This amusing tale is probably outrageous hyperbole but, whatever the truth, Erle did leave Corfe very quickly, but not before making one good decision, that of entrusting the fate of his men and ordnance into the relatively untested hands of one Captain William Sydenham. Francis's company of dragoons was also part of Erle's regiment at that time and would have certainly stayed with William at such a potentially dangerous turn of events. These two 'brothers in arms' would stay together until separated by death.

William, after quickly assessing the situation, decided to end the siege and head for the small port of Swanage a few miles to the east, fighting, as he withdrew, a superb rearguard action all the way there against the attacks from Maurice's men. No doubt, Francis and his troop of dragoons, specially trained mounted soldiers who could fight well on foot before re-mounting and riding off to fight again, played no small part in protecting the retreating roundheads. Once in Swanage, William commandeered several boats and effected a brilliant 'Dunkirk style' evacuation of his men and a few pieces of ordnance back to the forlorn Parliamentarian garrison at Poole, a few miles around the coast. He achieved this feat without the loss of one single soldier under his command, and this was to be a portent for his future brilliant military career.

Soon afterwards he is known to have raised his own regiment, his father lending him £559.00 on the 5th of July 1643. *"to enable him to wage war".* (Bayley 1910)[2]

The Roundheads allowed Mary Banks the honour of marching out with her colours flying as a mark of respect for her heroic stand.

---

[2] Unless otherwise stated, all quotations are from A.R. Bayley (1910) *The Great Civil War in Dorset.*

Commission of Colonel William Sydenham.

The enigmatic ruins of Corfe Castle in the Isle of Purbeck, home of 'Brave Dame Mary Bankes'. She held out for four years until 1646 when one of her own officers, a Colonel Pitman, betrayed her and let in the Roundheads to end the siege. A local legend says that as they advanced, she was reputed to have deposited all of the family jewels, gold and silver into a well and then ordered it sealed by exploding a barrel of gunpowder on top of it. It is said that the hoard remains undiscovered to this day. This magnificent early medieval fortress was then ordered to be 'slighted' (destroyed) by the Parliament so that it could never again be re-occupied by the Royalists. The task was beyond the besiegers however and it still stands today, bloodied but unbowed and is surely one of England's best known silhouettes. It even had an occupant as late as the nineteenth century.

4

The Plot to Betray Poole

Upon relieving Corfe, Prince Maurice eventually turned his gaze towards the *'little fisher town of Poole'* with it's very large useful harbour (the second largest natural harbour in the world) where William had sought refuge, but surmised that this garrison would not fall without a very stubborn and costly fight, both in terms of men and time. Instead he left to attack Exeter (via Dorchester) which had since fallen in to Parliamentary hands.

Before leaving he appointed one Ludovic Lindsey, the sixteenth Earl of Crawford, to wrestle with the problem of gaining the port for the King's cause and he too decided against an all-out attack due to the town's geography and stout defences. Instead he made his base at the nearby Royalist town of Wimborne, four miles to the north of Poole, where he chose to play a waiting game.

It was in the late summer of 1643 that Francis Sydenham, then a Captain of Dragoons, was quartered at the home of a leading Poole merchant, who was also well known as a Royalist sympathiser. Being owed money from various people living in the districts around Poole, the merchant gained permission from the Parliamentary governor of the town, Colonel John Bingham, for his wife to leave in order to try and collect some of his outstanding debts.

Upon reaching the town of Wimborne, the merchant's wife chanced to meet with a Cavalier officer by the name of Captain Thomas Philips. He, not unnaturally, quizzed her about the enemy garrison inside Poole and she, being of the Royalist persuasion, wasted no time in furnishing him with the answers he desired.

In reply to a question concerning the identities of the various Parliamentary officers in Poole, Philips seemed especially interested in her unwelcome lodger, Francis Sydenham. She told Philips that Sydenham was often heard bemoaning the financial losses that he had incurred since entering the service of the Parliament and this gave Philips the beginnings of a plan.

The Cavalier Philips asked the woman to enquire whether or not Francis Sydenham would meet with him at some neutral venue between the two warring towns, probably an inn, upon business of a mutually advantageous nature. It is a distinct possibility that the two men were acquainted before the outbreak of hostilities and that the King's man may well have confidently expected a favourable response to his request from the apparently unsettled rebel officer.

Upon her return, she did as she was asked, and Francis, his curiosity aroused, readily consented to the rendezvous. Obviously there was a considerable element of risk involved in such a venture and Sydenham, aware of this, took the precaution of secretly informing Governor Bingham of the situation before he left.

As Philips and Sydenham kept their appointment, the two men of noble birth must surely have been assessing the other's ability with the sword in case the mood should suddenly turn sour, but both would also be strictly adhering to the social conformities of their class in order to gain those things that they most desired from the meeting.

Eventually, Philips got around to disclosing the reason why he had requested the meeting. In short, he offered Francis Sydenham, for considerable financial gain, the opportunity to change sides and pledge his service thereafter to King Charles. Sydenham thought about it for a while and then insisted that he would only contemplate such a thing if he had all of the monies that he had lost in the service of the Parliament reimbursed to him and was also granted a free pardon. (The King considered all Parliamentarians to be rebels and traitors, whilst they, at the beginning of the war, mostly saw themselves as true and loyal subjects who were merely trying to protect their King from the evil counseling of those around him)

Philips assured him that both these demands and much more was possible if he would assist the Wimborne men in capturing the port of Poole for the Royalist cause. A date for a further meeting was agreed upon and the two plotters left to report back to their superiors, Phillips to Lord Crawford and Sydenham to the Governor of Poole, Colonel John Bingham.

The Cavalier, Thomas Philips, 'persuades' Francis Sydenham to change sides

A few days later, Francis received a sealed letter from Lord Crawford himself, promising a pardon and money as long as the town was delivered in to his hands. But Sydenham, an eye ever open for gain, wrote back saying that he would need some prior assurance of good faith before embarking upon such a hazardous course of action. Crawford, eager to not let this prized fish slip the hook, immediately sent the young dragoon officer the not inconsiderable sum of forty pounds via a Royalist spy, a Minister named Melledge, together with the sure and certain promise of much more to come.

In the days that followed, the plotters conceived a daring plan to the effect that on a certain night, not long distant, when Sydenham was to be the officer of the watch, he would cause the town gates to be left open and thereby allow a large Royalist force to enter and seize the town of Poole before the garrison could act to prevent it. The gates were situated at the end of the Sterte Road, (now sadly the site of a flyover) and was then, the only way into Poole by land. Even this was not straightforward however, as the road often flooded at high tide thus making the town a virtual island for part of the time. Also, moored next to the gates in the waters of what is now Holes Bay (but was then called Longfleet Bay) lay a Parliamentarian frigate with its guns perpetually trained upon the Sterte Road.

The plan called for this particular problem to be solved by Francis who, after opening the gates, would then have to board the ship and with the aid of a few trusted men, eliminate the crew and render the guns on board useless to the defenders. It was also agreed that the 'turncoat' Francis Sydenham would be allowed to keep the ship as part of his payment and also be given the rank of at least a Sergeant Major in the army of the King. All this agreed upon at a final meeting, Crawford then sent Francis a further one hundred pounds to seal the deal along with a suggestion that he *"appeared to all the world as adventurous as ever before to avoid any suspicions"*.

Francis Sydenham seemed to take this advice very much to heart and soon after; his troop ambushed a Royalist force escorting prisoners and commanded by a Lieutenant Colonel Verney. Several other officers and men were also captured along with a quantity of horses and arms later used in the defence of Poole.

Finally came the night when the plot was to unfold. Sydenham's men had the town watch and the tide was low so as not to hinder the advance of the Wimborne Royalists who numbered eight troops of Horse together with two regiments of the Marquis of Hertford's Foot commanded by Colonels Bernard Ashley and Conyer Griffin (or Griffeth). The Royal ranks were further swelled to about five hundred strong by a few sympathizers from the surrounding areas. As planned, the entire force was met about a mile or so from the town (probably at Stanley Green) by one of Sydenham's men, who assured them that all was well. The time was about two o clock in the morning.

As the Cavaliers crept ever nearer to the gate, Francis cried out *"All is our own, on, on"* and then blew upon a horn which he always carried. The Royalists, expecting just such a signal, rushed towards the gates, the Earl of Crawford among the first of them.

The gates had what was described as a half-moon feature that was raised by means of two chains and, as the ebullient King's men filled this space before the open gates, the chains were suddenly drawn up, trapping them within. Suddenly the ordnance situated on the town walls, together with many musketeers, opened up on the attackers slaying many where they stood, startled and ensnared. Somehow Crawford escaped injury and fled together with the remnants of his shocked and dispirited force back towards Wimborne, their plans in tatters and cursing the name of Francis Sydenham.

A pamphlet printed soon afterwards for the Parliamentarians by 'L N' for 'Laurence Blaikelock, to be sold at his shop at Temple Barre,' and sumptuously entitled 'A True Relation of a Plot to Betray the Town of Poole in the County of Dorset' declared that:

> *"All who were not slain threw down their arms and ran away, the arms which they lost for horse and foot were about 300. In the half-moon were taken near 50 horse, the riders escaping all but twenty which were taken prisoner."*

The Poole Roundheads later bemoaned the fact that they had mounted their artillery pieces too high, otherwise the slaughter would have been all the greater. The pamphlet went on to describe the body count as "Divers Cart Loads".

Poole was never again so seriously threatened and together with another Dorset town, Lyme, in the extreme west of the County, held the proud distinction of never once falling into Royalist hands throughout the whole nine year duration of the three Civil Wars.

As might be expected, Crawford's version of events and of the number of Royalist casualties differs somewhat from the Parliamentarian viewpoint. He claimed that:

> *"Only ten men were slain and four taken prisoner. The rebels durst not sally out upon the King's forces, who retreated safely to their quarters, leaving perfidious Sydenham to his perjury and treason to receive a just recompense with his fellow rebels, when he shall be less trusted and more exemplarily rewarded."*

In 1835 a skeleton was unearthed on the site by workmen engaged upon digging a well. It was assumed at the time that it was one of the fallen Royalists because the corpse sported long hair. In reality though, both sides mainly wore their hair long and also dressed similarly and it cannot be certain that the deceased was part of the ill-fated attempt to take the town in 1643.

5

The Sydenham Pedigree up to 1645

The following section is a chronological account of some of the more important events and engagements that occurred in Dorset and involving the Sydenham family. They all eventually lead up to the momentous, bloody and enthralling episode in Weymouth known as the Crabchurch Conspiracy.

May 1643: Francis Sydenham and his troop of dragoons ride to Shaftesbury to meet with Sir Edward Hungerford's regiment and assist in the storming of Wardour Castle at Tisbury, Wiltshire.

June 1643: The first siege of Corfe Castle in which Sir Walter Erle fled, leaving William Sydenham to save his command, a task which he was more than equal to.

August 1643: The plot to betray Poole where Francis Sydenham tricked the Wimborne Royalists into attacking the town, thinking that he would aid them and leave open the town's gates.

November 1643: The Parliamentarian Poole garrison sends out two hundred musketeers in a flotilla of boats commanded by Captain John Ley of Bridport. They made their way from Poole Quay to the River Frome or the Wareham River as it is known locally. The old Saxon market town of Wareham was in Royalist hands but after several skirmishes along the banks of the river and after also being taunted with the words *"now come of ye Roundheads if ye dare"*, the men of Poole succeeded in taking the town, *"being too wise for such untutored freshwater sailors"*!
A lovely example of local rivalry with Wareham port not being on the coast, but half way up the tidal river! Poole men did not consider Wareham men as real seamen and probably still don't!

December 1643: Francis Sydenham garrisoned Wareham and finding the inhabitants short of food, raided the Royalist-controlled 'Isle of Purbeck' stealing three hundred and twenty five head of cattle to feed the town. Later the same month he rode to Royalist held Dorchester at the head of one hundred men. He stormed the town taking prisoner Captain William Churchill (an ex Dorset Trained Bands comrade and now the Royalist Deputy Governor of Dorchester) along with his Lieutenant, Joseph Paty. Sydenham then broke open the Town's goal, releasing as many Parliamentarian prisoners as were inside, before heading back to Wareham.

On the return journey he intercepted a cart laden with muskets and gunpowder destined for the Royalist city of Bristol. Seizing it, he ordered the powder to be thrown in to a river and then smashed two hundred of the muskets, carrying off 80, that being all that his men could manage. Finally, nearing Wareham he came across a Royalist goldsmith called Robert Coker, relieving him of such gold and plate as he had. The whole operation was completed in 8 hours from start to finish and bears wonderful testament to this young Dorset man's zeal and energy in serving the cause he believed in. A zeal that was matched on both sides of the divide of course.

January 1644: A detachment of the Poole garrison ambushes Colonel George Wyndham's regiment from Wiltshire, killing a Lieutenant Barker and several common soldiers. Many prisoners were taken, Wyndham among them.

February 18th 1644: Now promoted to Colonel, William Sydenham's regiment rout the Irish Lord Inchiquin's troops somewhere near Poole, killing some and firing their magazine. Two pieces of ordnance and 8 prisoners are taken... Sydenham then decided to give the defeated Irishmen *"as much quarter as they gave the Protestants in Ireland"*.

One of the eight was given his freedom ... but only in exchange for performing the execution of his comrades ...

The man was forced to personally hang each of the other seven before being allowed to go free and to no doubt relay back to Inchiquin and his officers the strength of purpose inherent in the Dorset Parliamentarians, whose lands they hoped to subdue in the King's name.

The Earl of Essex was said to have backed William in his actions, declaring that the unfortunates were *"true papists"* and that he *"would have no quarter allowed to those"*. Such atrocities were alas, commonplace on both sides and outlined in the starkest manner imaginable, the religious differences of the time, sadly still with us today.

February 20th 1644: A Royalist convoy transporting arms to their garrisons at Weymouth and Melcombe was attacked and captured by soldiers from Poole and Wareham. It was also discovered that among the booty was a shipment of gold belonging to none-other than Prince Rupert, the King's favourite nephew. The Duke of Cumberland also owned a share of the hoard which was to be shipped to the continent and totaled upwards of three thousand pounds. It was duly confiscated and used by the Parliament men in the war against the King.

February 27th 1644: Captain Francis Sydenham at the head of three hundred troops encountered a numerically inferior Royalist patrol of just twenty horse and twenty five foot soldiers at Holmebridge, between Wareham and Wool. Again they were part of the Irish Lord Inchiquin's regiment and they took up a defensive position on and around an old bridge across a river. Obviously angry, and mindful of the sickening fate which befell their countrymen less than two weeks before at the hands of William, the Irishmen put up a very spirited defence for more than five hours, spurred on by their officer, Captain Purdon. Both he and his Lieutenant were seriously wounded during the engagement but insisted on being set down upon the bridge where they continued to shout encouragement to their troops.

Eventually Francis Sydenham was forced to withdraw, losing forty men killed and also leaving behind five cartloads of hay, earlier plundered from the countryside. Purdon's Lieutenant bled to death on the bridge as the contest raged. This action is evidence that the Sydenham brothers did not always come out as victors in their various tussles with the soldiers of the King's army.

June 11th 1644: A six thousand strong Parliamentarian army under the Earl of Essex marched into Dorset and William Sydenham is re-appointed as the Governor of Weymouth and Melcombe after the royalist garrison there, surrenders without resistance.

June 1644: A detachment of two hundred cavalry from the army of the Roundhead commander Sir William Waller were quartered at Blandford. However some citizens of that mainly Royalist town betrayed their presence to a much larger Cavalier force commanded by Sir Lewis Dyve some miles off at Sherborne. Before the Royalists arrived though, a Parliamentarian sympathiser warned them and all but twelve escaped capture.

As retaliation for this and also for *"betraying the many kindnesses shown to that community by the Earl of Essex and his men"* Francis Sydenham and Captain George Starr, the M.P. for Shaftesbury, rode to Blandford with a troop of horse and seized the Bailiff, Augustine Drake. They then allowed their men to ransack and plunder the town, before putting it to the torch.[3]

July 11th 1644: (A Thursday) Lieutenant Colonel Henry O' Brien, brother-in-law of Lord Inchiquin arrived outside Dorchester which was only recently

---

[3] Everyone remembers the terrible fire that burned Blandford to the ground in Georgian times, but few are aware of the one that did similar damage during the English Civil Wars.

liberated from Royalist hands by the Earl of Essex and demanded a ransom of one thousand pounds to not plunder the town. Arriving at seven in the morning he finally lost patience and attacked at two o clock in the afternoon. Unbeknown to O'Brien, the townspeople had managed to summon assistance from Weymouth and Melcombe. Before the help arrived they put up a brave resistance against the two hundred and forty Irish raiders, the women of Dorchester fighting alongside their men with anything that came to hand.

Eventually, Captain Francis Sydenham arrived with a relieving force and chased off the Cavaliers who rode back to Wareham, which was once more in the King's hands. Riding with Francis was the recently released Sydenham patriarch, his father, William and also the third Sydenham brother, Thomas. He had recently left his medical studies at Magdalen College, Oxford due to that city now being occupied by the King and his court, to join the Roundhead army as a Cornet in his older brother Francis's troop of dragoons. He was said to have *"behaved himself most bravely"* in this action. He was aged just nineteen at the time and went on to become the foremost medical mind of the entire 17th Century in the whole of Europe.

July 1644: Colonel William Sydenham becomes the M.P. for Melcombe.

August 9th 1644: Francis Sydenham, now stationed in Dorchester, beats off an assault on the town by Colonel Francis Doddington of the King's Army. Doddington was renowned for treating his prisoners very cruelly and on at least one occasion beat a Roundhead prisoner so brutally about the skull that he fractured it. The unfortunate man was then included in a batch of twelve that were hung in retaliation for William Sydenham's execution of Inchiquin's seven Irish soldiers. Doddington also once forced a father to hang his own son.

Dorchester had been described by the Royalist historian, Clarendon as *"the most malignant town in England, being entirely disaffected to the King"* (The Earl of Clarendon, 1807). The citizens of the town had, at the outbreak of hostilities in 1642, been very susceptible to the *'war-fever'* and propaganda that was so prevalent at the time. So much so in fact, that upon cornering two Catholic priests who had not obeyed a recent parliamentary proclamation requiring their kind to leave the country, that they decided to make an example of one of them and execute him. The other talked his way to a reprieve by recanting his religion.

The remaining priest named Hugh Green, was dragged to Gallows Hill, close to the modern junction of Icen Way and South Walks and on to the scaffold there. Once there, this unfortunate priest further infuriated the baying mob by insisting that he was not a traitor. He was henceforth hung, but as was the practice then, taken down before the rope had done its work and, as the rabble screamed for more sport, the local barber surgeon, Mathew Barfoot, aided and abetted by the hangman, then proceeded to cut out Green's entrails. Hopefully the unfortunate soul died from this outrage and was thus spared the pain of the next macabre act to be perpetrated against his person, that of cutting out his heart, which was then displayed on a pikestaff and finally, cast into a fire. Soon afterwards, the wretched cadaver was further mutilated by the dismemberment of its limbs and decapitation. The 'charming' audience then amused itself by using the head as a football for a while, before coming up with the notion of inserting sticks into the eyes, ears and similarly, the nostrils and mouth. The piteous object and its other constituent parts were then finally reunited by being unceremoniously interred nearby.

At this time many of the Parliamentarian persuasion saw Catholicism as almost the sole cause of the war in that they viewed the Queen, Henrietta Maria, herself a French Catholic, as trying to turn the King's head by gradually converting him to her religion, and thereby in time, bringing the whole country once more under the mantle of Rome.

6

The Siege of Abbotsbury House

In the first week of November, the Parliamentarian Field Marshall Sir Antony Ashley Cooper, (later the Earl of Shaftesbury) entered the old village of Abbotsbury, a few miles west of Weymouth, to call upon the Royalist garrison there to surrender. The three hundred strong garrison was ensconced in and around the old Manor House, the ancestral home of its commander, Colonel James Strangways and his father, Sir John.

Accompanying Cooper were the Sydenham brothers, but the union was not a happy one. William and Francis openly disliked and distrusted the Field Marshall as, at the beginning of the war, he declared his allegiance to the King. He later changed sides after a scheme that he had put before Charles to end the war backfired and left him looking rather foolish in his own County and the country in general.

Cooper was the nobleman, who in 1643 had persuaded many of the Parliamentarian garrisons in Dorset to trust him and let in various 'neutral men' to act as go-betweens towards an ending of hostilities. Melcombe was the first town in the county to honour the agreement and it was then (as mentioned in part one) that those unruly troops under Prince Maurice had entered the town and savagely pillaged it, thereby discrediting Cooper's scheme. Despite the fact that Cooper had then sent messages to the other Roundhead garrisons warning them to abandon his plan, this did not appease William Sydenham, who was then in his first tenure as Governor of the twin towns. He was consequently forced to relinquish them to the Royalists as a result.

Cooper called upon the Abbotsbury Cavaliers to surrender but as he reported, *"they hung out their bloody flag and returned a slighting answer"*.

The nearby church of St Nicholas also contained a small outpost of thirteen Royalist musketeers and Sir Antony ordered a Major Edward Baynton to lead an assault upon it. After a short time the soldiers inside the church were overwhelmed and once again the Parliamentarians summoned the

Strangways to *"surrender and yield on fair quarter, or else expect no mercy"* if they forced the Roundheads to attack.

Yet again a wholly uncomplimentary reply was received and so the siege began in earnest. Cooper and his men attacked the front of the old Manor House whilst the Sydenhams assaulted the rear. Cooper's troops first burned down the *"outgate to a court"* which was impeding their progress to the main part of the house, his soldiers then running headlong through the flames towards the hall porch, all the while under fire from the Royalist musketeers inside the old Manor House.

Once there, they also set the porch alight with bundles of *"furze faggots"*. These were a dried heath land plant used for fuel and feeding cattle.

The Parliamentarian musketeers then concentrated so much firepower upon the downstairs windows that the defenders in that part of the house were obliged to flee upstairs. Then the Roundhead artillery was brought in to play, blasting the side of the house with *"fire balls and grenadoes"* and after the bombardment, soldiers with scaling ladders tried to set light to the second storey. The royalist defenders were resolute though and succeeded in forcing them from their perches and so instead the Parliamentarians busied themselves with wrenching open the abandoned downstairs windows with iron bars and throwing in the faggots of burning furze engulfing the whole of the ground floor in flames. The now desperate Cavaliers tried frantically to extinguish the fire but were too late, and soon they were heard screaming for mercy as the inferno spread, creeping ever upwards through the stricken old building.

Having twice been spurned in his attempts to end the matter peacefully, Sir Antony was now in no mood to dispense clemency and decided therefore to make an example of the Strangways to other such royal garrisons in the County. At this juncture however the simmering rivalry between him and the Sydenhams boiled over and the brothers, attacking the rear of the house, began to offer quarter to their desperate foe.

It is certain that Cooper would have informed them of his decision to allow Strangway's garrison to perish in the flames and it must therefore be assumed that they openly defied his orders. Among the several possible reasons for their defiance could have been that they simply wished to antagonise Cooper, but equally likely is that it was done out of respect for their gallant enemy inside the house. However it is also known that a generation before, the Strangways and the Sydenhams were related by marriage, as an uncle of Sir John Strangways married one Ursula Sydenham and therefore links between the two Dorset dynasties were probably cordial before the outbreak of civil war.

The Sydenham brothers offering quarter to the beleaguered Abbotsbury garrison.

At the rear, the choking Cavaliers were allowed to jump and scramble to safety, unmolested, from the upper storey of the now doomed building before being taken prisoner and one of the reprieved Royalists repaid the Sydenham brother's kindness by warning them that the garrison's magazine was about to explode and that it would be advisable if nobody dared to enter the house in search of plunder. Many of the common soldiery of Ashley Cooper's and Sydenham's regiments refused to heed the warning however and ran in to the building anyway to grab a prize for their troubles. Arrears of pay in this war were commonplace and plunder was a very viable means of making ends meet, both for officers and the ordinary soldiery alike.

As foretold, a huge fireball soon ripped through the old house giving those who had ventured inside little chance of survival as the deafening explosion also rained down lumps of deadly masonry on all who stood nearby. At least forty Roundheads were killed including a Captain Heathcock and a Lieutenant Kennet whilst eighty more that were standing in the courtyard were *"lifted a yard from the ground by the blast"*. Cooper estimated the number to be nearer sixty. Among the very few inside the house who survived the explosion was a Lieutenant Hill who had volunteered to enter the building in an effort to try and persuade the looters to leave. He was pulled barely alive from the debris as the house crumbled and burned. It was also reported that a Captain Gorge, *"a very gallant young man, was hurt in the head with a freestone from the Church Tower and shot through the ankle"*.

Sir Antony Ashley Cooper later wrote about the six hour siege and below is his account in his own words:

Honourable,

Yesterday we advanced with your brigade to Abbotsbury as a place of great concern, and which by the whole council of war was held feasible. We came thither just at night, and sent them a summons by a trumpeter, to which they returned a slighting answer and hung out their bloody flag. Immediately we drew out a party of musketeers, with which Major Bainton in person stormed the church, into which they had put thirteen men because it flanked the house. This, after a hot bickering, we carried, and took all the men prisoners. After this we sent them a second summons under our hands that they might have fair quarter if they would accept it, otherwise they must expect none if they forced us to a storm. But they were so gallant that they would admit of no treaty, so that we prepared ourselves to force it and accordingly fell on. The business was extreme hot for above six hours; we were forced to burn down an outgate to a court before we could get to the house, and then our men rushed in through the fire and got into the hall porch, where with furze faggots they set fire on it, and plied the windows so hard with small shot, that the enemy durst not appear in the low rooms; in the mean time one of our guns played on the other side of the house, and the gunners with fire balls and granadoes with scaling ladders endeavoured to fire the second story, but that not taking effect our soldiers were forced to wrench open the windows with iron bars, and pouring in faggots of furze fired, set the whole house in a flaming fire, so that is was not possible to be quenched, and then they cried for quarter, but we having lost divers men before it, and considering how many garrisons of the same nature we were to deal with, I gave command there should be none given, but they should be kept into the house, that they and their garrison might fall together, which the soldiers with a great deal of alacrity would have performed, but that Colonel and Major Sydenham, riding to the other side of the house, gave them quarter, upon which our men fell into the house to plunder and could not be by any of their commanders drawn out, though they were told the enemy's magazine was near the fire, and if they stayed would prove their ruin, which accordingly fell out, for the powder taking fire blew up all that were in the house, and blew four score that were in the court a yard from the ground, but hurt only two of them. Mr. Darby was of the number, but not hurt. We had hurt and killed by the enemy not fifteen, but I fear four times that number will not satisfy for the last mischance. Captain Heathcock and Mr. Cooper (who did extremely bravely) were both slain by the blow of the powder. Captain Gorge, a very gallant young gentleman, is hurt in the head with a free stone from the church tower and shot through the ankle, but we hope will live. Lieutenant Kennett to Major Peutt, who behaved himself very well, was blown up with the powder and slain, and Lieutenant Hill, who went a volunteer and was sent in to get out the soldiers, was blown up with the rest, yet since we have taken him strongly out of the rubbish and hope to preserve him. The house is burnt down to the ground and could not be saved. We have prisoners Colonel James Strangways, Major Coles, and three captains, besides a hundred foot soldiers and thirty horse, all Strangways's whole regiment. Sir William Waller's officers all of them behaved themselves extreme gallantly, and more than could be expected in their readiness and observance for your commands; we cannot say to whom you owe most thanks, only Lieutenant Colonel Oxford we are extremely obliged to for his nobleness in joining this expedition though without command, only on our entreaty. Captain Starr and Captain Woodward behaved themselves extremely well. Our men are so worn out with duty and this mischance, that we are necessitated to retire to Dorchester to refresh them. If you have anything in particular to command us we shall most readily obey you. To-morrow we have a council of war of all the officers, and then we shall conclude of what may be of most advantage to your service, and by God's blessing will faithfully prosecute it. Colonel Sidenham has yet afforded us no ammunition; all his men are supplied from us hitherto besides. He makes not up his Regiment either of horse or foot, he has withdrawn one more company this way. We have given him orders that all the prisoners that are officers shall be sent to you. We humbly desire you will be pleased to consent to no exchange for any of them till Haynes (Colonel Heane) be exchanged.

A.A. Cooper

After the battle of Abbotsbury, it was decided that the Sydenhams would escort the prisoners into captivity at Dorchester, but history records that the Commander of the beaten royalist garrison, Colonel James Strangways, never made it to Dorchester gaol. Somehow he managed an escape en route and thereafter made his way across the Channel to France. Whether this was with the connivance of the Sydenham brothers, cannot be proven, but from the available evidence, including the act of mercy on the previous day, these soldiers of opposing armies and ideals, probably held each other in no small regard and so, it is a possibility that Colonel James Strangways' escape, was something to do with the Sydenham brothers. Though of course, this cannot be proven.

The church of St. Nicholas still stands today and inside is a wonderful carved Jacobean pulpit, which is shot through with two musket ball holes as proof of Major Baynton's attack upon the building prior to the main siege.

Sir Antony Ashley Cooper was furious that the Sydenhams had wantonly disobeyed his orders to let Strangway's garrison perish in the flames and afterwards wrote to the County Committee demanding that William and Francis be stripped of their commissions and their regiment disbanded.

Their response could not have left him more displeased, as it recommended, on the advice of none other that Sir William Waller himself, that William Sydenham be henceforth made Commander in Chief of all Parliamentary forces in Dorset instead of Cooper and furthermore, that Francis be put in sole command of all the Parliamentary cavalry in the County.

Cooper was also responsible for the jailing of Sydenham's father in Exeter for several months in 1642. A fact that would have enraged the brothers still further and made them determined to punish the former Royalist turncoat if the opportunity to do so ever materialised.

And as is often remarked, 'Revenge, is a dish best served cold'.

The approach to Strangways Manor (probably the "outgate to a court", mentioned in the account).

The remains of Strangways Manor house.

The Strangways private doorway in to the Abbotsbury church.

Detail of the date on the Strangways private entrance.

The Jacobean pulpit in Abbotsbury church, shot through with two musket-ball holes.

November 17ᵗʰ/18ᵗʰ 1644: Francis Sydenham, now commissioned as a Major, accompanied members of the Parliamentary garrison of Lyme in an attack upon Royalist held Axminster in Devon. The town was put to the torch.

November 30ᵗʰ 1644: The King's commander in Dorset, Sir Lewis Dyve, suddenly appeared outside the gates of Poole with three hundred cavalry and dragoons. Francis Sydenham being present in the town at the time with his own troop of horse and *"weary of an enemy who suddenly vanished like a vaporous cloud"*, gave chase after realising that one of their number was none other than Major Williams, a Royalist dragoon officer who had led a raid upon the Sydenham family home at Wynford Eagle three months earlier. This intrusion in itself could have been overlooked in the context of the times and was almost to be expected, but as far as the Sydenham brothers were concerned, Williams was already a dead man walking. The reason being that he had, during the raid, callously murdered their mother as she defiantly barred him and his raiders entry to her house. He slew her in cold blood upon her own doorstep in the old stone porch of Wynford Eagle Manor.

Drawing out only sixty of his finest horsemen, *"double pistolled"*, Francis rode straight out of Poole in single-minded pursuit of his mother's murderer Williams, chasing him and his comrades all the way to Dorchester (twenty three miles), which had yet again fallen to the King. Once there Francis Sydenham turned to his men and cried; *"Give the dragoons no quarter and stick close to me, for I shall now avenge my mother's innocent blood or die in this place".*

Charging headlong at the numerically superior Royalist force and *"beating them back through the town"* the Roundheads regrouped and charged for a second time. Francis Sydenham, cold vengeance his only spur, grimly hacked his way through the Cavalier ranks until at last he was face to face with Major Williams. Aiming his pistol, he fired. The ball struck the murderer square in the forehead and he fell down dead beneath his horse's feet.

Sir Lewis Dyve was also "sorely wounded" in the initial engagement outside Poole.[4]

December 1644: Possibly mindful of why so many of their own men had died at Abbotsbury, Francis Sydenham took his troop up to London and set up an encampment outside the Parliament, refusing to leave until his men were given their arrears of pay.

His men were eventually paid in full, before they left.

---

[4] It has been suggested that Major Williams was possibly John Williams of Plumber, 3ʳᵈ son of John Williams of Herrington. A Gentleman called John Williams, the heir to the Herringstone estate and keeper of the King's game for the Royal Manor of Fordington. had stabbed a tapster to death at the George in Dorchester in 1623 and fled abroad, but used his wealth to gain a pardon.

Soon after, he joined his brother William as part of the garrison inside Weymouth and Melcombe, no doubt expecting a reasonably peaceful winter in what seemed to be, a now secure parliamentarian stronghold.

But, in times of civil war, things are not always as they appear.

"Give the dragoons no quarter and stick close to me, for I shall now avenge my mother's innocent blood or die in this place".

7

The Crabchurch Conspiracy

February 1645 Weymouth: In the days and weeks following his re-appointment as Governor of Weymouth and Melcombe, William Sydenham set about the task of thoroughly strengthening the defences of both towns, but especially Weymouth which was probably more open to attack than its neighbour. Soon the garrison and townspeople seemed to slip into a comfortable state of ease with each other, or so it appeared. This is borne out in the invaluable writings of the local minister, a staunch Parliamentarian and probable Puritan preacher named Peter Ince whose observations about life within Weymouth and Melcombe at this time are an invaluable source of research. (A full transcript of his diary may be found at the back of this book, written exactly as he penned it)

Ince wrote:

> "In the beginning of February 1645 we were in as sweet a quiet and security as any garrison in the Kingdom; no enemy near us but one at Portland, and that not very considerable, being but about three hundred or four hundred men."

The total number of Parliamentarian troops in both towns was then about nine hundred souls, as besides Sydenham's men, another Roundhead unit, that of Colonel Ralph Weldon was also present from the January of 1645 and so, Ince's assertion that Sydenham's garrison was secure and in no immediate danger would seem to be correct.

The Portland Royalists to which Preacher Ince was referring in his diary were commanded by Sir William Hastings, who had long been casting an interested eye towards Weymouth. And his prayers seemed to have been answered when one day; a woman arrived on the island at his headquarters in Portland Castle, a channel defence fort built during the reign of Henry VIII. At first he was dubious as he listened to what she was imparting. Her name was Elizabeth Wall, a Weymouth woman and she seemed to be telling Hastings that she was part of an intricate plot being hatched in the twin towns by certain leading citizens, loyal to the King's cause. Their avowed aim was to deliver the ports back into the hands of the Royalists at the first available opportunity.

She was a widow, the daughter of Mistress Thomazine Dennis, and her husband may have been slain by the Roundheads in the war. But any doubts that Hastings may have been harboring about her motives, honesty or sanity were soon dispelled however when she suddenly produced a 'tongue token'. These were tiny oval shaped gold coins with the monarch's head stamped on one side and his initial on the other and were only given by high-ranking Royalists to their most trusted of messengers. The logic being that if stopped and searched by the enemy, the coin could be easily concealed under the tongue to avoid detection, thereby preserving their proof of identity when they finally presented themselves at their destination. Hastings needed no further proof of her sincerity and began to listen more intently as she made him aware of the details of the plot that had been developing, a plot that he was now destined to play a major part in.

It transpired that the leading Melcombe councilor and merchant named Fabian Hodder was the chief architect behind the conspiracy. Together with his wife and other citizens such as John Mills, the Weymouth town Constable, John Cade, an ex-Royalist sea-captain and a local fisherman named Walter Bond they hoped to achieve the goal within a few weeks. They had already secured an assurance of help from Sir Lewis Dyve, the King's commander in Dorset, whom Elizabeth Wall had previously visited in Sherborne a day or two before and it was Dyve who had given her the tongue token to ensure that Hastings was compliant towards the aims of the conspirators.

The plan was nothing if not audacious. Hastings' men were to launch a surprise attack and take the two main forts of Weymouth and in doing so, gain control of the town and its seaward approaches, whilst at precisely the same time; Dyve would attack and overwhelm the garrison inside Melcombe. All this was to be achieved with the connivance of the various conspirators from within the two towns who would act as guides, 'door openers' and assassins where required.

The two main forts on the Weymouth side were the Nothe Fort, a structure situated on an isolated promontory or knoll, jutting out into Weymouth Bay and whose guns watched over the harbour entrance, and secondly the far more powerful Chapel Fort of St. Nicholas. This was situated on a hill above Weymouth quayside, in what is now the Chapelhay area of the town. As its name suggests, it was a defunct 14th century church which the Roundheads had fortified strongly and surrounded with 'outworks' (defensive banks and ditches). Subsequent messages between Sherborne and Portland were delivered by Elizabeth Wall and a date and time, Sunday the 9th February at midnight, finally agreed upon when the two Royalist forces would rendezvous to destroy Sydenham's garrison and once again give control of one of England's most important ports to the King's cause.

It has been suggested that the King, Charles 1, intended to land a huge French Catholic army at the ports once the plot had succeeded, with which he hoped to turn the tide of the war once more in his favour. The likely price of such assistance, could well have been that England once again became a Catholic country as many feared it might.

Sir Lewis Dyve must have particularly relished the idea of avenging himself upon the Sydenhams, not only because of the injuries he sustained when Francis chased and killed his mother's murderer to Dorchester, but also because his wife, Howarda, happened to be the daughter of Sir John Strangways, the patriarch of the now destroyed Abbotsbury House.

The plan called for the fort on the Nothe headland to be attacked by a sea-borne force from Portland who would be guided to their target by the Weymouth fisherman, Walter Bond. He was to land them at Newton's Cove near the foot of the fort. The more powerful and strategically important Chapel Fort of St Nicholas above Weymouth quayside was to be assaulted by a second Portland contingent who would be met at the ferry crossing known locally as 'the passage'. This was the stretch of water between Portland and the small fishing village of Wyke on the mainland. Their guide was to be John Dry, a Weymouth tanner, who would take them through the sparsely populated hinterland with its rural lanes and track ways towards their objective.

Dyve's task was to simultaneously attack Melcombe, having first been let in to the town through a 'side door' by one Thomas Samways. The remaining conspirators would then cause as much chaos as possible from within, whether by attacking Sydenham's soldiers when the opportunity arose or, by starting small fires to keep them occupied as Dyve's men crept in to the town.

At about 5pm on the appointed day, the Royalist soldiers of the Portland garrison gathered in the castle together with many of the island's tough fishermen and quarrymen, heavily armed and determined to succeed. Hastings and his officers then selected about a hundred and twenty men for the mission, who were then split in to the two equal groups of sixty.

It had been agreed with the plotters that the Cavalier side should tie a white cloth to their sleeves as a 'field sign' so that when the fighting began, friend would hopefully not slay friend in the midnight darkness. A password, 'Crabchurch' was also agreed upon as a further aid to identification and was chosen because it was the name of an ancient area on the east side of the Isle of Portland.

The leader of the conspirators, Fabian Hodder spent the day in question trying to bribe as many of the townspeople as he thought could be trusted to take up arms and fight for the King once the fighting started. Although he used the considerable inducement of five pounds per head, a princely sum at that time, he got few takers apart from some gunners in the Chapel Fort and must have wondered whether he would be given away at the final hurdle by one of those that he had approached. It is interesting to note, however, that of those who refused Hodder's offer, none saw fit to warn the Parliamentarians either of the ensuing attack; presumably because of the fear of reprisals should the plot still be successful. Those who did accept the offer were obliged to swear an oath on the Holy Trinity not to betray the undertaking, Oaths being of supreme importance and a matter of personal honour in the seventeenth century.

Fabian Hodder and the plotters toast the success of the Crabchurch Conspiracy.

At eight o clock that evening, many of the 'Crabchurch Conspirators' gathered for a final time at the house of one of their number, William Philips, who lived just beneath the Chapel Fort, possibly in the old High Street of Weymouth. (This area is now sadly, a council office block and car park, but some vestiges of the dwellings still remain for the inquisitive to find, including old stone fireplaces and private steps leading from the backs of the houses to the former Chapel on the hill and the Chapelhay area in general)

The plotters probably drank a toast to the success of their scheme and put their fate into the hands of God before leaving to make their way to their allotted places and tasks. Some of the other men present included :- John Seton, Leonard Symonds, Walter Mich, John Lock, Philip Ashe, Samuel Tackle and Thomas Samways, the tailor from Melcombe who was to be the means of access into that town for Dyve's party from Sherborne Castle.

As the final hours ticked away and the two groups of Portlanders made their way towards their destinations, another group just as determined to serve their King, waited in Radipole Meadow, a mile or so to the north of Melcombe. They were Royalist sympathisers from various nearby villages such as Upway, Broadwey, Sutton Poyntz and Preston. They numbered about sixty and were led by John Fieldew, but were in the main, poorly armed with *"cudgels, various farming tools and possessing but two pistols between them."* Among their number who had all accepted Hodder's five pounds were :- John Bryer, Alexander Butcher, Edward Flatman, Thomas Coxe, John Antony, William Willsheere, Andrew Galshell, Robert and John Bower and John Meech (the younger). They were to link up with Sir Lewis Dyve and his party from Sherborne in the meadow and were then to dispose of the sentries on the main gate in Melcombe, ahead of Dyve's attack.

Eleven o-clock came and went, then half eleven. The villagers anxiously scanned the freezing darkness with streaming eyes and their ears numbed with cold, whilst the grass around their feet had long since turned white with frost. But still Dyve did not appear.

Midnight, and far off could plainly be heard the sounds of battle. Musket-shot rent the still night air as the resolute Portlanders pressed home their attacks upon the two main forts of Weymouth. The frustration of the royalist villagers must have been almost too much to bear as, even if Sir Lewis Dyve and his party did turn up now, the element of surprise would have been lost to them and the Roundhead garrison inside Melcombe, would be on their watch and wondering what on earth was happening just across the water on this cold, dark night.

Walter Bond and his sea-borne party easily took the Nothe Fort and those attacking the Chapel Fort were also successful, totally surprising the few sleepy guards there and infiltrating the main part of the building before any organised resistance could be put together. The startled Parliamentarians fled, disorientated into the dark unlit streets of old Weymouth below, not knowing what to do next. One man however had not lost his senses. Suddenly, Major Francis Sydenham appeared from his billet down in the town, shouting commands and somehow organising the ousted soldiers into a cohesive fighting unit again. Within an hour he was leading his men back up the hill towards their former stronghold and as ever, Francis Sydenham was leading from the front.

The position was fiercely contested and the Parliamentarians were determined to regain the fort, but the Portlanders had used the hour's grace to good effect and organised an equally strong defence. Gradually the Roundheads were beaten back, but as the fighting finally subsided, an altogether bigger blow became apparent. Their talisman, Major Francis Sydenham was down and, he was badly hurt.

His distraught men carried him back down into Weymouth, but a few hours later at dawn, he succumbed to his wounds and died, aged just twenty seven years. He left a wife, Mary and two small children, William two, and tiny daughter Frances, aged one.

Preacher Ince afterwards wrote in his diary:

> *"Among the slain was Major Francis Sydenham, the Governor's brother, whose memory may not be buried with him. His death was no small joy to his enemies, to whom he was a perpetual vexation and terror … and no small grief to us who had our eyes too much upon him"*

This heart-felt epitaph to a fearless and dedicated Dorset soldier speaks volumes for his character and sadly, marks the end of such a promising and courageous young life. His brothers William, Thomas, John and Richard would all go on to make a mark in their chosen fields of endeavour and we can only surmise as to what Francis would have achieved had he not met his untimely end on the heights of Chapelhay, just another victim of the Crabchurch Conspiracy.

"Our eyes too much upon him" Major Francis Sydenham received a fatal wound whilst leading the counter-attack upon the Chapel Fort.

Although never actually stated in the official records of the time, it is interesting to note that on contemporary maps, Chapelhay Street which leads up to the site of the fort, was for a short time during the Interregnum (the period of Cromwell's Commonwealth) called 'Francis Street' It is entirely feasible that this was done to mark the spot where this much respected officer met his end and that this fact has since been forgotten. In all likelihood, the name would have been changed back to Chapelhay Street at the time of the Restoration of Charles II. He visited the County in 1665 after his court had moved to Salisbury to escape the Plague which was then ravaging the capital. Upon a visit to Poole on the 15th of September 1665 it is said that he ordered the wall around the town to be demolished as penance for their rebel stand against his father.

Across the water in Melcombe, William would obviously have heard the sounds of battle and would have ordered that the drawbridge on the bridge linking the towns be raised, in case Weymouth fell to the enemy. But no such outcome was possible in Melcombe. The final vital part of the conspirators plan had failed to reach fruition with the conspicuous absence of Sir Lewis Dyve and his fifteen hundred men who should have attacked William Sydenham in Melcombe. The Royalist villagers in Radipole Meadow who had waited for him had long since dispersed and gone to their beds by the time that the routed Roundheads of Weymouth had started to make their way across the water as best they could or overland via Westham, to join their comrades in Melcombe.

Among their number was the young Cornet Thomas Sydenham, himself wounded and possibly bearing the body of his beloved brother Francis. Sir Lewis Dyve did finally enter the scene on the following day at around noon. He and Sir William Hastings finally mopped up any lingering resistance in Weymouth, killing or taking prisoner those soldiers of Sydenham's and Weldon's regiments who did not make good their escape under cover or darkness.

8

The Siege of Melcombe

Colonel William Sydenham now had a very sizeable problem to wrestle with. He had less than nine hundred men under his command in Melcombe and was faced across the water by an ecstatic enemy now numbering in excess of two thousand troops; an enemy who would not long be content to sit and do nothing. Mourning the loss of Francis, perhaps the two remaining Sydenham brothers present gained an inner strength from his example and resolved to reverse their fortunes. But above all, they desired with all their hearts to avenge themselves upon his slayers.

Three days after the 'surprise of the forts', it is recorded that a number of Cavaliers took themselves off to an area near Radipole called Causeway, where along with a Master Wood, the clerk curate of Sutton Poyntz they *"regaled themselves at an alehouse and became distempered with beer"*.
Sadly though, for the besieged Parliamentarians within the town of Melcombe, not all of the King's men were occupied thus, as the ever trusty pen of Preacher Ince relates. He wrote: *"A multitude of great bullets and iron bars, hot and cold poured in to Melcombe, some of their gunners engaged themselves to level us with the ground"* A protracted and internecine siege had begun as the two sides began to bombard each other with what ever came to hand. However, the King's men, Dyve and Hastings, secure in Weymouth, had the massive advantage of having the much higher ground and specifically, the guns of the Chapel Fort and the Nothe Fort which were now perpetually trained upon their enemy. And this advantage eventually began to tell as they continually pounded the lower town of Melcombe causing great damage and injury and reducing many buildings there to rubble.
William Sydenham had decided to make a fight of it though and soon he was answering in kind. A fierce two way bombardment ensued lasting several days. Eventually Sydenham sent Dyve a message saying *"let us cease this useless burning"*, but Dyve believing he had the upper hand for once answered *"we refuse to parley with you and will do what we please"*.

This snub only served to infuriate Colonel William Sydenham and the very same evening under cover of darkness, he sent a small raiding party across the water in boats. They set alight several vessels and houses on the Weymouth side and caused great damage and mayhem in the Royalist camp. The next day Sir Lewis ceased the bombardment for good.

A tangible glimpse of the almost week long artillery duel can be seen in the wall of a seventeenth century house in Maiden Street, in Melcombe. These days the downstairs is rather strangely, a public toilet, but high up beneath the top window, is lodged a cannonball and the fabric of this lovely building can clearly be seen to be damaged around the point of impact.

The present ball is apparently not the original missile however, but a wooden replica, the real one being removed for safety sake. Local legend has the ball being fired from the fort on the Nothe, though it is quite possible that is was fired from a royalist ship which could have chanced its luck and got in whilst their side held the Nothe Peninsula during February 1645.[5]

The following week offered some hope to Sydenham's men in the shape of two hundred sailors from Poole who were landed on Melcombe beach by none other than William Batten, Vice Admiral of the Parliamentarian fleet, in his ship 'The James' and one other man o' war. Batten described the Poole seamen as *"some of the toughest fighting men in Dorset"*. Also, by land, came another reason for hope. Lieutenant Colonel James Heane (or Haynes) managed to break through the surrounding Royalists with his one hundred strong troop of horse. Heane was a good professional soldier, but had for several months been held prisoner by William Hastings in Portland Castle. His 'host' had tried hard to persuade his captive to change sides, realising that Heanes' superior military skills would be a real bonus to the King, but to no avail. Heane, a staunch Parliament man, eventually escaped with the help of Hastings' own servant and now returned to once more defy his jailer.

---

[5] A few years ago following a landslip in the Chapelhay Gardens in Weymouth which are situated directly below the site where the Chapel Fort once stood, a rough hewn stone cannon ball was found buried. Could this have been evidence of William Sydenham's desperation to defend his command, having run out of the more conventional iron variety of cannon shot?

'The cannonball in the wall', Maiden Street, Melcombe Regis. Said to have been fired from the fort on the Nothe Headland during the siege of Melcombe, (but I think it more likely that it was fired from a Royalist ship in the harbour).

The cannonball being shown to acclaimed English Civil War historian and author, Professor Ronald Hutton, by Crabchurch author, Mark Vine.

Colonel William Sydenham was beginning to feel more confident now and on Sunday 16th of February 1645, even ventured out of Melcombe with a troop of horse and succeeded in routing a unit of Royalist cavalry near Radipole, killing some and capturing forty five prisoners and eighty horses. He then *"chased the little remnant that remained up to the gates of Weymouth"*. Soon after, Dyve, with a detachment of Sir Thomas Austin's and Cleveland's horse and some companies of foot, tried to blockade the Roundheads in at the north end of Melcombe, but still Sydenham's raiders managed to break out on several occasions. Once they returned with nine hundred sheep to feed the town and also a rather bewildered and no doubt embarrassed Cavalier captain, who had mistaken the Roundheads for his own side and rode up to greet them!

These halcyon days were but a brief respite though and soon enough the Parliamentarians' luck began to take a downward turn once more, with the dire news that the infamous and much feared Royalist General, George, Lord Goring was approaching Dorchester. He was the typical Cavalier of fable, a loud, flamboyant 'peacock' of a man, but nevertheless a very experienced officer of national renown who had an ego every bit as big as his reputation. His soldiers were dreaded by all, due to their unfortunate habit of heartlessly plundering and vandalising every town that they entered. Once in control of Dorchester and true to form, they were duly let off the leash and ran riot, destroying among other things the 'brew-house' run by one Benjamin Devenish.

Goring's force was made up of three thousand cavalry and fifteen hundred infantry and, once he had established himself in Dorchester, he headed straight for William Sydenham at the head of three thousand troops. Panic rang through the war ravaged streets of Melcombe as Sydenham's garrison, already outnumbered by two to one, looked out upon the massive body of soldiers now marching to join those already encamped outside their walls.

Goring paraded his men up and down in a great show of strength with drums beating, trumpets blowing and flags waving, but, astonishingly, did little else. Instead of the expected onslaught, Sydenham and his men watched with some relief as Goring eventually marched off again towards Weymouth, where he spent the night as Dyve's guest, leaving only a token force behind to dig an artillery position about two hundred yards from Melcombe, possibly somewhere between the present library and the northern end of Great George Street.

Sydenham, making the most of this reprieve, decided to provide a little show of his own and early the next morning, bombarded Goring's newly dug 'works' and, in the true family tradition, followed this up by throwing open the town gates and personally leading a cavalry attack upon it, killing several of the defenders and capturing many arms and tools.

A further two days passed but still Goring did not attack. Probably convinced in his own mind that the town could be taken at leisure, he had apparently returned to Dorchester with most of his number, having made his first mistake, that of underestimating Colonel William Sydenham.

At about mid-day on the 25th of February 1645, two weeks after the siege began, Sydenham was informed that a party of Royalist horse was escorting several wagon loads of supplies into Weymouth, and he decided to send out a troop of his own horse to attack the convoy in the hope of capturing a wagon or two of much needed food. It is possible that the wagons were sent by Goring himself as a gift for Dyve, and the two groups clashed somewhere near the little village of Westham, to the west of Weymouth.

Incredibly, Sydenham's horsemen succeeded in completely routing the entire royalist escort, who fled in disarray off towards their comrades in Weymouth, leaving the Roundhead victors to try and turn the wagons about and head for the comparative safety of Melcombe with their prize. Sir Lewis Dyve had been observing this lamentable turn of events from high up in the Chapel Fort and was so livid that he immediately dispatched more than a hundred of his infantry from Weymouth off towards the scene of the disaster to try and remedy the situation.

This understandable, but ill-conceived, reaction proved to be the turning point of the whole campaign, for as soon as Dyve's men were far enough away, Sydenham immediately ordered that the drawbridge separating the two towns be lowered. He then sent one hundred and fifty of his own musketeers, led by a Major Wilson and a Captain Langford, charging headlong across the bridge and onto Weymouth quayside, sweeping all before them in an unstoppable wave of musket balls and bravado. Storming onwards and upwards through the outworks and on into the Chapel Fort of St. Nicholas itself, they soon defeated the weakened Royalist defenders who, possibly believing that the Roundheads had more men than they actually did, broke and fled in the face of this fierce brand of hand to hand fighting that Sydenham's men had taken to their very doors.

Within half an hour it was all over and the powerful Chapel Fort of St Nicholas, regained by the parliamentary side and with it, all of Weymouth. At least six Royalists were killed during this action, among them one of the original 'Crabchurch Conspirators', Philip Ashe, and upwards of a hundred prisoners taken, including *"a Lieutenant Colonel, a Major, three Captains and three Lieutenants, the rest being inferior officers and common soldiers"*.

One of the Captains was a local man named Alexander Keynes, who owned Radipole Farm and whom Preacher Ince describes as *"a Papist having in his portmanteau a parcel of holy beads, and a commission for a ship to play the pirate with at sea which lay blank at Dunkirk"*.

William Sydenham was later granted the use of Keynes' farm and all produce from it for one full year, after it was 'sequestered' (confiscated) by order of Parliament. It also appears that Keynes may have had more than a little to do with organising the villagers who gathered in Radipole to meet Dyve on the night of the initial Royalist attacks upon the two forts, as they were known to have been at Radipole Dairyhouse which he owned, earlier that evening.

The most vivid account of what the hapless Cavaliers were up against on the 25th of February 1645, comes from one of their own men and could be considered an unbiased account. Richard Wiseman was a surgeon with Lieutenant Colonel Ballard's Regiment and tended the Royalist wounded in Weymouth during the fifteen days that the King's army held it after the conspiracy.

In the years after the war he would carve out a commendable niche for himself in the annals of British medical history, becoming known as the 'Father of English Surgery'.

He wrote:

> *"As Sydenham's troops attacked I was dressing a wounded man in the town almost under Chapel Fort and hearing a woman cry, "fly- the Fort is taken", I turned aside a little amazed towards the line not knowing what had been done, but getting up the works I saw our people running away, and those in the Fort shooting at them. I slipped down this work into a ditch and got out of the trench; and as I began to run hearing one call ' Chirurgeon', (surgeon) I turned back and seeing a man hold up a stumped arm, I thought it was an Irishman whom I had absolutely dismembered, whereupon I returned and helped him. We ran together, it being within half a musket shot of the enemies Fort, but he outran me quite".*

Proof then of the rapidity with which William Sydenham lifted the siege of Melcombe and regained the Chapelfort and town of Weymouth.

Wiseman's journals provide other gems describing life and death as it was in the Weymouth garrison during those desperate days and although some descriptions are clearly not for the squeamish, they are however as fascinating as they are gruesome and a wonderful insight in to the work of a front line medical man of the period. For example, here he describes how he treated a Roundhead soldier who had been shot in the foot and captured at the initial surprise of the forts on the 9th February 1645.

"A great haemorrhage happening to a soldier at the surprise of Weymouth by the garrison of Portland, by a shot through the heel, I endeavoured the stopping of the blood, by astringents bandages etc. But after all I was put to the use of actual cautery (cauterising) *which I did successfully apply."*

Another passage describes the lamentable fate of another soldier, again an Irishman of Wiseman's own regiment. It graphically demonstrates the dangers of being wounded during these and any wars of the time and the grisly end which so many poor souls had to endure. He writes:

"At the siege of Melcombe, an Irish soldier of Lieutenant Colonel Ballard's, which by the grazing of a cannon shot, had a great part of his forehead carried off, and the skull fractured in many places and some of it driven with the hairy scalp in to the brain. The man fell down as dead, but after a while moved, and an hour or two after, his fellow soldiers seeing him endeavour to rise, fetched me to him. I pulled out the pieces of bones and lacerated flesh from amongst the brain in which they were entangled and dressed him up with soft folded linen dipped in Caphalick Balsaam, and with emplaster and bandage bound him up, supposing I should never see him anymore.
Yet he lived seventeenth days, and the fifteenth day walked from the Great Fort over against Portland, to the bridge which separates Weymouth from Melcombe only led by the hand of some of his fellow soldiers. The second day after, he fell into a spasmus and died howling like a dog, as most of those do who have been so wounded."

The castle mentioned by Wiseman was possibly Sandsfoot Castle at Wyke, another of Henry VIII's channel forts and which was designed to work in tandem with Portland Castle opposite in protecting the entrance to Portland Harbour. It was used as a Royalist mint for a time, the now rare coins produced there, bearing an 'S' on their flan.

The remains of Sandsfoot Castle, Wyke Regis, a former Royalist mint, with the Isle of Portland in the background. In June 1643 as a huge twelve thousand strong Roundhead army under Robert Devereux, the Earl of Essex approached it's walls, the six Cavaliers inside took several hours to decide whether or not they should surrender to it!

Sydenham now had not one, but two towns to defend and only about twelve hundred soldiers under his command with which to do it. Dyve barely escaped capture at the fall of Weymouth and he and his surviving men made their way to Dorchester, where he would not have relished having to relate to Lord Goring exactly how he managed to lose a baggage train *and* the town of Weymouth in one rash moment.

Whilst there, Dyve wrote to his stepfather, The Earl of Bristol, concerning the matter, calling the loss of Weymouth *"a strange misfortune"*, but continued in a surprisingly upbeat manner.

> *"My Lord Goring hath set up his rest to go through with it, being confident of your speedy assistance in a work of that infinite importance to His Majesty's service so that this place (Weymouth & Melcombe) being taken, which we are confident cannot be a work of many days, the West is not only secured thereby, but my Lord Goring will likewise have an opportunity of advancing into the associated counties, which are now left naked".*

From Dyve's correspondence then, it is plain that Goring was more determined than ever to deal harshly with the Sydenham problem. He had always planned to attack and take Melcombe, but now the impudence with which William had acted, called for a lesson in total warfare, a lesson that the provincial upstart, Colonel William Sydenham, would never forget.

9

The Battle of Weymouth

William Sydenham had no idea when or indeed where the attack would come, he only knew that it was inevitable, and he made such preparations as he could to strengthen the defences of both towns in whatever time he had left to him. On the morning of the 27th February 1645, the ever reliable Vice Admiral Batten once again sailed in to Weymouth Bay and landed a further one hundred men to add to Sydenham's twelve hundred souls, but this would still leave the Roundheads outnumbered by almost six to one. It is unlikely that the small three hundred strong, predominantly Irish, Royalist garrison of Lord Inchiquin's at the Nothe Fort would have fired it's cannons at Batten's vessels, as they were probably feeling rather isolated since the fall of Weymouth and therefore would not be over keen to draw attention to themselves until relief came.

In the early evening of the 27th of February 1645, a troop of Sydenham's cavalry who were patrolling at Upwey, a couple of miles north of Melcombe, to watch for any signs of Goring's army, came across an escaped Parliamentarian soldier. The man, who had been captured about three days before and held in Dorchester gaol, was trying to make his way to the twin ports with a devastating tale to tell. The cavalrymen quickly transported him to Colonel William Sydenham, and the escapee anxiously told him of a conversation he had overheard between two guards, a conversation about an imminent attack upon Weymouth and Melcombe, that very night. This gave the Roundheads only a matter of hours to speed up their preparations for defence and Admiral Batten readily agreed to stay and fight in the ensuing battle. As midnight approached, the beleaguered garrison of the twin towns prepared themselves for a fight to the death and wondered who among them would live to see the dawn.

The Old Town Hall of Weymouth on the right of this picture, seen here in its present rebuilt condition with the old Boot Inn opposite. This was the scene of some of the heaviest fighting during the Battle of Weymouth and the stonework at the front of this magnificent building is peppered with musket, carbine and pistol shot.

The road to the right of the Old Town Hall is Chapelhay Street, which leads up to the site where the Chapel Fort of St Nicholas once stood. It was this road which was renamed, Francis Street after the civil wars, possibly in honour of the fallen Sydenham brother, Francis, who was killed somewhere in this area following the initial surprise of the forts on the night of the 9th February 1645.

The original bell from the time of the Conspiracy was recently returned to the Weymouth Old Town Hall and, at time of writing, is waiting to be re-installed in the tower by the small, but dedicated band of volunteers who are refurbishing it and intend to open a Weymouth Old Town Heritage Centre based upon the Crabchurch story and the Sydenham family.

As foretold, Goring, with his vastly superior force appeared in the vicinity of the towns at around midnight and immediately split his force into two factions. That portion of his men, who were given the task of attacking Melcombe, somewhat inexplicably did little more than sit behind a bank and almost half-heartedly fire a few shots at the defences, but the fighting across the water in Weymouth where William Sydenham had positioned himself was of a very different calibre indeed.

Behind the Town gates which were situated near the western end of Boot Hill, just past the Boot Inn, the Parliamentarians had hastily erected a barricade stretching roughly from the bottom of Chapelhay Street, in front of the old Tudor town hall and across to the Boot Inn. (both buildings happily still exist today)

Realising that the Town Gate and this barricade would soon be overwhelmed through sheer weight of numbers, Sydenham had set up another defensive position at the other end of the narrow old High Street which led up to Boot Hill. At the far end of this street were seventy stone steps dating from medieval times that led straight up to the Chapel Fort should they be needed as an escape route, and always assuming that the fort had not fallen to the enemy by then, as it too was under attack from Goring's soldiers.

As expected, the gate and the first barricade soon fell, and the Parliamentarian defenders duly melted away into the darkness of the bitter winter night and took up their positions with others at the eastern end of the old High Street almost opposite the present day lifting bridge, deep inside Weymouth town. Goring's jubilant cavaliers swarmed over the abandoned obstacles and rushed headlong down the narrow, unlit High Street, baying for blood and convinced that an easy victory and welcome revenge would soon be theirs.

The Old Boot Inn, a probable officer's billet in the civil war which found itself in the front line during the Battle of Weymouth and is now one of the most popular hostelries in the town.

A stone 'gate pillar' first recognised by local writer and historian, Debby Rose as a housing for one side of the old town gate that Goring's forces attacked and broke through on the night of the Battle of Weymouth. Despite being asked to list the feature, English Heritage has refused, saying that there is not enough evidence to support the listing. This, despite being shown an excerpt by Debby Rose of a line from the Town's minutes of 1655 stating ... "Love Lane end, by the west gate" The pillar is exactly in line with the aforementioned Love Lane and of course, the entry was made ten years after the battle.

On they came in their hundreds and as they approached the second position, Sydenham gave the order to fire. Several concealed cannon, together with countless musketeers who were stationed at every window, rooftop and doorway, poured a withering wall of deadly lead shot and iron ball in to the Royalist ranks. Confusion reigned in the enveloping darkness and the stench of black powder and blood hung thick in the chilled night air. The numerous Royalist dead and wounded at the front of the advance were trampled underfoot by their stumbling comrades, who were still streaming down from the other end of the street in large numbers, if not oblivious to what had occurred then certainly not realising the extent of the disaster and slaughter.

These are quite possibly the recently re-discovered seventy stone steps' that lead up to Chapelhay from Weymouth quayside and which Sydenham was determined to protect and make use of if his plan to beat Lord Goring failed. He wrote that he "resolved to make good so much of it (the town) as might let us, upon any occasion, to and from the Chapel Fort". His trap would have been set a few yards to the right of here at the bottom of the old High Street. These steps, which are situated in the back garden of a shop on North Quay match up exactly with the course of the old rope ferry across to St. Nicholas Street, in Melcombe and lead right up to the site of the Chapel Fort of St. Nicholas following a continuous line. They could even possibly have been another location where Francis Sydenham was mortally wounded. These days they are covered with thick foliage and have a later, brick wall dividing them in two, but without the brick wall, the steps become quite a substantial historical feature.

Not content with this carnage, Sydenham's Dorset soldiers then drew their swords or upended their muskets to use as clubs and rushed out to get to grips with Goring's men at close quarters. A deadly hand-to-hand struggle developed as the Royalists fought desperately to extricate themselves from the trap. Eventually, Goring's men broke and ran, Sydenham's troops chasing them back up the old High Street and all the way out of Weymouth town.

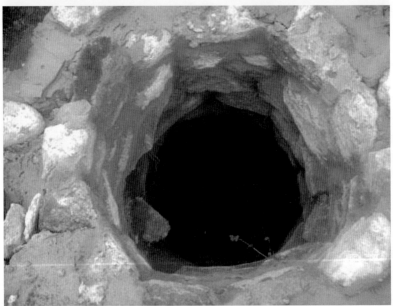

A recently discovered well, possibly Medieval in origin, which is situated at the bottom of the stone steps to Chapelhay and is as yet unexcavated.

Elsewhere though, the battle was far from won. Above, the Chapel Fort was also under fierce assault and the contest there could still go either way and now, the reluctant Irish garrison at the Nothe had suddenly found new heart and was fighting its way into Weymouth from the east at Hope (Ope). Their efforts were rewarded and soon they had attacked and occupied a small fort in the heart of Weymouth, situated on the quayside near the bridge which led to Melcombe.

The old High Street of Weymouth as it is today. It was down here that Goring's troops confidently charged on the night of the 27th February 1645, but were in effect, being funneled into Colonel Sydenham's deadly trap. The foliage on the right still contains some remains of the backs of the original houses, such as fireplaces and steps etc and above, at the far end would have been the site of the Chapel Fort of St Nicholas.

Sadly the other side of the street was completely bulldozed away during the rampant days of philistine planning decisions in the late nineteen sixties, early nineteen seventies. Sickeningly, the High Street was reputed to have been one of the most complete rows of Medieval and Tudor buildings in Britain at the time of its destruction.

The magnificent old Tudor House, Number 4 High Street, wantonly destroyed along with the rest of the old Weymouth High Street by Weymouth Council when building a nice new office block for themselves in the late 1960s and early 1970s. The Council invited Princess Anne along to open it and the highlight of the day...was a mock Tudor banquet! The irony seems to have been lost on them.

Sydenham had ordered that the bridge be destroyed in case one of the towns fell and put the other in jeopardy. The fort taken by the Irish troops was commanded by a Captain Thornhill, who is thought to have been an uncle of the celebrated Weymouth-born artist, Sir James Thornhill, who was in fact, one of William Sydenham's grandsons and the first ever artist to be knighted. He painted the ceilings of the dome of St. Paul's Cathedral, the Greenwich Hall and Blenheim Palace and was reputed to have been born in what is now the White Hart Inn, in Melcombe which still survives today (2013) though in a much altered state.

The White Hart, Melcombe. Reputedly the birth-place of the celebrated Dorset artist, Sir James Thornhill, the first ever artist to be knighted.

As Thornhill's soldiers were ousted by the Nothe Irishmen and made their getaway, they were met by Sydenham and his triumphant troops coming up from the battle in the nearby High Street. He persuaded them to turn and fight and eventually, together they managed to eject the Irish contingent from the Town Bridge fort.

The Irishmen retreated in some disorder back the way they came; hoping to get to the comparative safety of their own fort upon the Nothe headland. But here also the rout was to turn into another disaster for the unfortunate King's army.[6]

The now rampant Colonel William Sydenham and his men mercilessly forced the Irishmen back along Weymouth quayside. But, in those days, the area which is now solid ground beyond Trinity Street near the Old Rooms Inn through to Hope Square at Brewers Quay, was then nothing more than an

---

[6] At the beginning of this book is a map of Weymouth and Melcombe from a nineteenth century copy of a seventeenth century original, which shows that the bridge at the time of the Crabchurch Conspiracy was in the same place as the present day one. Only once, in 1770, did a bridge span the Quays in a different location and this, the last of the wooden bridges, went from St Nicholas Street in Melcombe Regis across to Weymouth's North Quay, but only lasted for fifty years before being replaced by one built once more from St Thomas Street.

inlet filled with cold, deep water, known as 'The Hole'. In the frosty darkness of the small hours, and gripped with blind panic due to the ferocity of Sydenham's charge, most of the luckless Nothe men blundered in to, or else were driven straight over, the quayside and into the icy February waters below, where those that didn't immediately drown were easy prey for the Roundheads. As many as two hundred and fifty souls perished in a few grisly minutes. Colonel Sydenham's horse was literally shot and killed beneath him as the chase ensued and turned to carnage for the men from County Clare.

The Irish Royalists either blundered into, or were driven, into the icy February waters of Weymouth quay by Sydenham's men.

War damage to stonework on Pilgrim House in Hope Square, Weymouth. The house itself was rebuilt in the 18th century, but Geologist and Civil War ballistics enthusiast, Brian March, believes that the stones bearing the damage are original and from the civil war period. He further believes after studying the damage, that the missile which caused it was fired from the small fort at Bincleaves and were "a mix of hail shot and solid rounds from a standard nine pounder cannon".

With Melcombe hardly being challenged by the Royalists at all and the Parliamentarians defending the Chapel Fort of St. Nicholas finally succeeding in repelling their assailants, the Battle of Weymouth was all but over. Colonel William Sydenham had achieved a near *"miraculous"* victory against overwhelming odds and Lord Goring and his surviving soldiers took themselves off to the small village of Wyke to lick their many wounds and ponder the fortunes of war.

The almost annihilated Nothe garrison, together with another small Cavalier garrison in a fort at nearby Bincleaves, made good their escapes, not even bothering to *"spike their guns",* so as to make them unusable to the Parliamentarians, nor caring to take their colours with them. Sydenham's victory over Goring and Dyve was total and complete, with only the Isle of Portland still remaining in Royalist hands locally.

Excellent written evidence exists of the amazing events of the night of February 27th 1645 in old Weymouth. Both Sydenham and Batten composed graphic letters in the days directly after the battle and these correspondences demonstrate wonderfully what occurred there. First, Sydenham wrote the following account two days after the battle (March 1st) in a letter to the Parliamentary Committee of the West. He begins with how he first regained Weymouth.

> *"Having now some few hours of freedom, from those continued sallyes, alarms, firings and batteries which almost these three weeks have kept me from the least leisure to do anything, but attend the enemy, I think it my duty to give you an account of God's miraculous dispensations towards us. All (as you have formally received) being treacherously delivered in to the hands of the enemy except Melcombe.*
>
> *On Tuesday last, February 25th the enemy having drawn out many of their foot to relieve a party of their horse, being in danger to be engaged by a party of ours which I sent out to discover the enemy. I fell presently upon Weymouth, which town (together with the Chapel Fort) was in an hour regained, where we took prisoners, one Lieutenant Colonel, one Major, three Captains and one hundred of inferior officers and soldiers, which so enraged the enemy that upon Thursday last about midnight they furiously stormed us at several places in both towns. Out of all Weymouth we were not able to keep them, and therefore resolved to make good so much of it as might let us, upon any occasion, to and from the Chapel Fort.*
>
> *The enemy came in great multitudes through the streets and backsides at both ends of the town, and disputed with us very hotly about three hours for that small part of it, which we were willing to keep. The Chapel Fort, and Melcombe being likewise stormed at the same time from all which places God enabled us to repel them. In all this time they wounded but one of my men.*
>
> *What execution is done upon the enemy, I am not certain, they carrying off as many as they were able before day, amongst whom (as the people of the town have since informed me) were divers in buffe coats and velvet jackets. They left much blood behind them in the streets and slain men upon the place, they carried (as it is reported) many wounded men into one village a mile from the town (Wyke)".*

During the whole 17 days of fighting, Sydenham maintained that he actually only lost about ten men killed and, if this is true, then he may have had some justification in claiming that God was indeed on his side, though how many more subsequently died from their wounds is not known. However, he still expected Goring to make another assault and near the end of his letter describes the enemy as *"still blocking us up as before"*, and *"what they mean to do next I know not, but do expect some further design upon us."*

His concern was, in the end, unfounded. A large Parliamentarian army under Sir William Waller was rumoured to have entered the County and further proof of Goring's intentions are provided by Vice Admiral Batten in a letter written soon after Sydenham's. It confirms that Goring and his men had eventually fled off towards Taunton in Somerset, *"in a very confused manner"*. He also reported that:

> *"I have two of my own company, one hath lost a leg, the other dangerously wounded and will hardly escape. And three of Captain Jordan's men scalded by a mischance, by the firing of some powder".*

Batten wrote another letter on the morning directly after the battle (28th February), whilst on board his ship 'The Reformation', moored in Weymouth Bay. Here, he refers to the great losses inflicted upon the Irish Royalists who had held the Nothe Fort, and also makes a deserved reference to Sydenham's character and qualities of leadership. He wrote;

> *"At night a prisoner of ours ran from them, who gave us notice that they would storm the town that night, in all places that they could, which was performed accordingly, the enemy getting within our works near to Weymouth Bridge, but were gallantly repulsed by our men with the loss of some hundreds of the enemy. The Governor* (Sydenham) *himself behaving himself like a gallant man as he hath done in all the siege".*

With the Royalist threat finally gone, it was now to be a time of vengeance for Colonel William Sydenham. Vengeance upon those who had hatched the Crabchurch Conspiracy and in doing so caused him to lose a much loved brother and comrade in arms.

Now those people would have to pay the price.

10

The Executions on the Nothe

After a Council of War, attended by the Captains of the Garrison and Vice Admiral William Batten on the 1st March 1645, William Sydenham convened a court of enquiry and soon most of the plotters names and the parts they played in the conspiracy were known to him. The arch-plotter, Fabian Hodder, had already made good his escape but was arrested near Poole and thrown in to the jail there to await the time that William Sydenham came to get him. Most of the others who had not fled or perished in the fighting, were put safely into the hold of Batten's ship to await their fate, a fact that he remarks upon in his wide-ranging correspondence. He wrote of his prisoners that they were *"in a posture, speedily to be hanged"* and later:

> *"Tomorrow we shall shorten the number by hanging some of the townsmen on board us and were the betrayers of the town".*

In the two days leading up to the trials, several depositions were recorded from various people in and around Weymouth and from their evidence, eventually, confessions were made by two of the leading Crabchurch Conspirators, Captain John Cade and the former Weymouth Town Constable, John Mills. Those depositions can be read later in this book.

Besides Philip Ashe, at least two other Crabchurch conspirators lost their lives during the fighting. They were Leonard Symonds and William Philips, who owned the house beneath the Chapel Fort where the plotters met for the last time on that fateful night of the 9th of February 1645. Amongst those being held on the ship were Walter Bond, the Hope Fisherman, Thomas Samways, the Melcombe Tailor, John Mills, the Weymouth Town Constable and John Cade, the ex-Royalist sea-captain.

Another man, who must have played an important role in the deadly plot, was also held with them, but he was never to make it to trial. His name was Richard Mighill, one of the original gunners at the Chapel Fort and a known friend of the conspiracy's chief messenger, Elizabeth Wall. He was for some reason, thrown out of Parliamentarian-controlled Weymouth prior to the plot and went to live on Royalist Portland. Given that this man was previously a gunner in the Chapel Fort, he would almost certainly have drawn a map of the fortifications for the attackers and, may even have been one of the sixty from Portland who took the fort, acting as a guide once they arrived at the Chapel Fort defences.

Mighill was a native Irishman and that fact alone would have weighed heavily against him, as Sydenham had already shown how ruthlessly he was prepared to deal with that race a year before (February 18th, 1644) when he hanged seven of them and his mood certainly had not improved towards them since then. So much propaganda abounded concerning real and supposed atrocities committed by indigenous Irish Catholics against English and Scottish Protestant settlers in Ireland that many zealous English Parliamentarian officers in the wars wasted no opportunity to mete out what they viewed as retribution in kind to any Irish caught in England fighting for the King.

According to the pen of Preacher Peter Ince, Richard Mighill committed suicide in the hold of the ship on the night before his trial and was *"an Irish rebel, a native papist who put a rope about his own neck and hanged himself ...without judgement or execution, doing all upon himself"*. We can only suppose that like so many others on both sides, Mighill's last hours on this earth were absolutely wretched.

The court of enquiry continued and ordered the arrests and questioning of all of those villagers who had waited in vain in Radipole Meadow for Sir Lewis Dyve on the first night of the conspiracy. However, after being given a severe reprimand by William Sydenham, they were eventually allowed to go free, probably due to the fact that they had not physically taken part in the assault.
Others though were not nearly so fortunate.

On the 3rd of March 1645, just four days after Lord Goring's over-confident and disastrous attempt to take the twin towns, the first of the plotters to feel the wrath of Colonel William Sydenham met his end upon the Nothe Gallows. Captain John Cade was hanged by the neck, as Ince put it *"after making a full confession of his crimes"*.

Next to appear before the assembled Roundhead garrison and the equally ragged townspeople were Walter Bond and Thomas Samways.
The pair stumbled unsteadily past the foot of the scaffold where Cade's body still swayed; limp in the cold March breeze and the charges were read to them. At that point though, the nerves and dignity of both these man

deserted them and they fell to their knees and began to beg for mercy before Sydenham and the court. Possibly seeing a chance to win over the local populous once and for all, Sydenham eventually relented and the two men were once more taken back to jail to, as the Parliamentarian propaganda paper, Mercurius Britannicus, put it *"make a further discovery of their partners"*.

Bond and Samways beg for mercy beneath the Nothe gibbet as Preacher Ince addresses the crowd.

Last up was the Weymouth town Constable, John Mills, a very brave man who was made of sterner stuff. A contemporary Pamphlet describes how this resolute soul managed to perform one last defiant gesture before his watching accusers.

> *"He most desperately, without any sign or token of sorrow or repentance, when he was upon the ladder, desperately threw himself off not showing any signs of humiliation or calling upon God, for mercy on his soul, but carelessly, in a most desperate manner died, not so much as praying to God to receive his soul".*

Ince finished his account of the executions by saying:

> *"There be not many of the villains left, as their sin hath found them out, divers of them are slain, Fabian Hodder and others are in prison at Poole and other places, not yet tried, and some are run away".*

11

Dyve's Revenge?

William Sydenham swore that he would have revenge upon the main architect of the Crabchurch Conspiracy, Fabian Hodder. Safely locked up in Poole Gaol, it was now only a matter of time before the arch-plotter and Melcombe merchant found himself transported back to the scene of his infamy. But before this could be achieved, Sydenham and Dyve had exchanged several letters on the subject. These two old protagonists fought each other just as hard with words as they ever did upon the field of battle.
It appears that for some reason, Dyve took it upon himself to try to preserve Hodder from the noose. Two of the letters amply demonstrate the simmering rivalry, hatred and sheer contempt that Sydenham and Dyve had for each other. The first is from Sir Lewis and is in answer to one already received from William.

For Master Sydenham At Waymouth:

In your last civil letter, which your trumpeter brought to me, you charge me with treachery, and Fabian Hodder and his wife for intelligencers and traitors. Look but upon your own heart, and there you shall find that character clearly written, where with you falsely and injuriously accuse of other men. The desire I had to preserve their innocence from your barbarous inhumanity, was for that I knew their approved loyalty to their sovereign was a crime sufficient to make them expect the worst of ills, from a traitor's hand.

But do your will, and heape vengeance on your own head, by shedding more innocent blood. Paty shall die, deservedly by the law of arms; having quitted the King's service, wherein he was entertained, and turning rebel. And whereas you threaten others of a higher orb shall follow him, know this, that were all my children under the power of your cruelty, I would not be diverted from justice to save their lives. And, for conclusion, be best assured that, if you put to death these innocent persons, I will vindicate this blood to the utmost of that power wherewith God shall enable me, upon you and yours without ever giving quarter to anyone who hath relation to you, which shall faithfully be performed by him that professeth himself your enemy.

Lewis Dyve, Sherborne, the 12th March 1645.

Dyve seems to be holding prisoner, a man called Paty and this is almost certainly the same Joseph Paty who was captured by Francis Sydenham in his raid on Dorchester in December 1643.

Paty was then a Royalist, but seems to have deserted the King's cause and changed sides due to an unknown dispute with Dyve. Unfortunately for him, he also seems to have got himself captured by his former comrades and was to be executed for his change of coat under the 'Law of Arms'.

Sydenham may have been bargaining the life of one of the conspirators for that of Paty, whom he probably knew before the war, but this would definitely not have been Fabian Hodder who, as we shall see in William's reply, was well beyond any hope of reprieve if the Roundhead soldier from Wynford Eagle had anything to do with it.

The strongest image from these letters is the absolute certainty with which both men argue their cause and believe theirs to be the more just. Sir Lewis Dyve could not possibly comprehend the reasoning behind any man ever raising his sword against their rightful King who was, in his opinion, chosen by God to rule, and he threatened to execute any of Sydenham's family who fell into his clutches. Sydenham, in answer, displays a sarcastic and witty character, no doubt honed by the success that he has recently achieved over his foe. In his letter he also demonstrates a firm understanding of Latin.

Pestes Humani Generis = 'The plague of the human race'
Heu Nefas Infandum = 'Alas, an abominable crime'

Here is Sydenham's reply:

For Sir Lewis Dyve these, at Sherborn Lodge:

You call my last letter 'civil', and yet you seem to be somewhat angry at it; which I should admire, had I not lately given you sufficient cause, for I must confess ingenuously, had I livery and seizon of your castle, I should not be so soon dislodged without some indignation, especially if an army of mine own party (viz Goring's) stood by and looked upon it. You desire me to look upon my own heart; which I have done, and find written there, in the fairest characters, a true desire of advancing God's honour,

maintaining the King's just power, and contending for the privileges of the
Parliament at Westminster, and the liberty of the subject; which when I
find you so maliciously opposing and despitefully stiling treason and
rebellion, I am induced to think this age hath produced unparalleled
monsters, which are (without slander) 'pestes humani generis', for traytor
I may not call you, which cannot possibly be guilty of such a sin in the
opinion of 'Aulicus' the only author which (it seems by your language)
you are versed in.

You are very tender of shedding innocent blood, and therefore Paty must
die; but good Sir Lewis, for what crime? He served, you say, on your
side; I have heard 'tis (as you do) only as a scribe; and hath since turned
rebel, because he would not tamely stand still whiles you were plundering
him. 'Heu nefas infandum'! for this, right or wrong, the poor man must
suffer, (and setting honesty aside) you will be just for certain.

May it please your worship to be merciful too, if not to him, yet to me and
mine (when we fall into your hands); till when your last experience might
remember you that I am as far from fearing, as my present condition is
far from needing your quarter, which I hope I shall have an opportunity
to dispute further of with you; whom to any man in England, I shall
answer in this quarrel. In the mean, know that I intend to make a halter
of your letter to hang Hodder with; whose crime is the first contrivance of
that treachery, which you after (tho, blessed be God! but simply) acted to
the loss of what you valued worth a crowne.

Paty you may hang, but will not be able to bury; which may occasion a
great mortality amongst you. And therefor be advised to forebear, by him,
to whom proclaiming yourself a professed enemy, you have invited me as
professedly to subscribe myself.

Yours W Sydenham.

Sydenham's firm, clever and even chilling reply portrays the confidence of a
man who knows that he has won the game. He has defeated Dyve at every
turn and now feels justified in taunting him about it.

Dyve's letter is dated the 12th of March 1645, a full nine days after the
execution of Cade and Mills, and Sydenham is still very confident of bringing
Hodder to book. The threat to *"make a halter of your letter to hang Hodder with"*,
must have infuriated Sir Lewis and may possibly have stirred him into
positive and immediate action on behalf of the condemned conspirator,
whose family was influential enough to warrant him being treated, if not as
an actual equal, then at least as more than a commoner by Dyve.

It is not possible to know exactly how, but one thing is certain, Fabian Hodder never did keep his appointment with William's hangman. Somehow he managed to escape from the gaol at Poole. He was, by the standards of the day, a fairly wealthy man and it is possible, though unlikely, that he bribed his way to freedom.

Or could it just be that Sir Lewis Dyve, a man of far greater wealth and influence than Hodder, shook the right hands after 'crossing them with silver' and whisked the conspirator away from a certain death upon the scaffold in Weymouth, thereby achieving a victory over William Sydenham in a way he never once managed to do upon the field of battle ?

This is pure conjecture of course, but it is not beyond the realms of possibility when considering all the other intrigues that are connected with this incredible story.

Hodder's family was visited by at least one more disaster however before the wars ended. It is recorded that a John Hodder, a younger brother of Fabian, took a man called John Vincent to court in 1649. Vincent was a potter from the tiny village of Broadwey, which lay two or three miles north of Melcombe on the road to Dorchester. John Hodder accused the potter of stealing a vast quantity of money and goods from him during the aftermath of the Crabchurch Conspiracy, four years before.

The younger Hodder, obviously being privy to what was about to occur care of his brother's 'activities', thought it wise to move most of his wealth away from the area of the twin towns until the fighting had subsided. He quite rightly feared being plundered by whichever side was to prevail and so struck a deal with Vincent who agreed to hide Hodder's possessions in his own home in Broadway until it was safe to retrieve them. Hodder told the court:

> "In the time of the late war when the West Country was oppressed with the soldiery, I handed Vincent the following articles and monies. (This being November 1644) "£175.00 in money, two silver beer bowls worth £9.00, one great silver beaker worth £5.00, four dozen silver spoons worth £16.00, a sugar dish of plate worth 20 shillings, a gilt silver bowl worth 35 shillings and 14 gold rings worth £25.00 together with two silver dishes, five silver spoons, a wine bowl, a silver whistle and chain and other articles".

Vincent's version of events was that he did indeed bury the said items on behalf of Hodder in various places in his house, but that in "February 1645, when the late King's forces rose their siege" of Melcombe, some of the defeated Cavaliers had plundered his house on their way back to Dorchester, digging up the floors and taking away all of Hodder's property except for twenty two shillings and sixpence, which Vincent found in the dirt the following morning…

Sadly, the reference neglects to reveal in whose favour the court found, but one thing is certain, if William Sydenham knew of this case, he must have worn a very broad smile for some time afterwards. For, either the Hodders had been robbed by Vincent, a trusted friend, or else by the very side that they had struggled and schemed so hard to install in their town, a few of whom had seemingly found out about the location of John Hodder's hoard. Whatever the truth of the matter, one thing is certain, as a direct result of the Crabchurch Conspiracy, a deadly plot of their own invention, the Hodder family had lost a very considerable portion of their personal wealth.

However, others of their acquaintance lost much, much more than that.

12

After the Fighting

Gradually, the citizens of the twin towns tried to return to some semblance of normality, but the enormity of the damage wrought by the conspiracy to the actual fabric of the communities, especially Weymouth, soon became only too apparent. So much earth had been extracted from around the houses for the building up of the various defensive works around the town that many buildings quite literally started to fall down through lack of firm support underneath.

Colonel William Sydenham: "My soldiers, horse and foot have all had very hard service of it day and night."

Colonel William Sydenham, at last had time to gather his thoughts and to do something positive for the fighting men of his own garrison who had served him so very loyally throughout the traumatic events of the eighteen days and nights of fighting and bloodshed wrought by the Crabchurch Conspiracy. He wrote to the Parliamentary Authorities saying:

Worthy Sir,

Since my last (perceiving the enemy received a party of my horse and theirs, having been lately engaged, and foot on each side to their assistance) I fell on with about a hundred and fifty Musketeers in the middle of the day, regained Weymouth and Chappell Fort, and tooke one Lieutenant Colonel, three Captains, three Lieutenants, and one hundred common men with store of provisions which the enemy had newly got by then, and all with the losse of but one man of ours, This did so enrage the enemy that the Lord Goring would needs be served, and to that purpose advanced with his whole body on Thursday night, and fell upon us about midnight at severall places, but entered only one of our Barricadoes, whence our men were beaten back, just as I came by, which perceiving, I got a fresh party and beat them off, recovered that foot, which was Captain Thornhills and killed and took some of the enemy there, This night we gave them such a brush, that Sir James Frampton of Buckland (Ripers), reported yesterday, that two of their regiments were spoiled, besides what they left in the street, and in the sea, it's reported that eighty dead men were carried into Wick, upon which (perceiving it seemes no good to be done by them, in keeping longer on the north, (Nothe) which we valued not when we had the Chappell, they suddainly stole out yesterday and have left both Beincliff (Bincleaves) and the North Forts, without either burning the Corne or houses or spayking our guns, which admire.

Thus miraculously hath God wrought for us in preserving this little disadvantageous place against the other Towns and Forts, and an Army, and which is more in giving us such success, and at last the possession of all in the face of that Army which cause to relieve them.

*I hope (whatsoever we have rescued, that this will ***** the Cavies, and hath (in detaining that body here which might have done mischiefe elsewhere) much advantaged the publique; God bringing food out of so ill My soldiers, horse and foot, have all had very hard service of it day and night, I shall treat you to write to the Parliament for something for their encouragement. They have neither money nor clothes, and yet unwearied in this business.*

Your affectionate servant,
W. Siddenham

On the 4th March 1645, an order was given by both the Lords and Commons for a 'Public Thanksgiving' to be held on the twelfth of that month (the same day that Dyve wrote his letter to Sydenham) and the Parliamentarian broadsheet, 'Mercurius Brittanicus', reported that:

> *"divers orders passed for payment of monies to the garrisons of Lyme, Weymouth and other places. But especially let Lyme and Weymouth be remembered by more gallant action. May we always remember the famous services of Sydenham and Ceeley.* (Governor of Lyme). *May they be a pattern of imitation to others in like cases of extremity."*

(Parliamentarian held Lyme's own story of siege was every bit as incredible and praiseworthy as Weymouth's, but I could not do their story justice here, so will not try. They were besieged by the King's nephew Prince Maurice. But that is for another writer)

A month later, a warrant was issued for the clearing of the war debris that littered the two towns. They were never again threatened by the King's army and remained under Parliamentary control until the wars finally ended in 1651, with the defeat of the last sizeable Cavalier army at the Battle of Worcester. Most of the forts of Weymouth and Melcombe were eventually dismantled after that. One is still remembered in a street name today. Blockhouse Lane which runs from St Mary's Street, east, towards the beach, led to the Blockhouse Fort.

The great Chapel Fort at Chapelhay Heights suffered a similar fate to the smaller ones, despite desperate pleas from many of the townspeople to rebuild it. Its stonework was sold to one Peter Wall for ten pounds and five shillings, possibly a relative of Elizabeth Wall who carried the conspirator's letters ?

The whereabouts of at least one piece of the Chapel Fort is known however. It is a chunk of pillar and was, until its closure recently, situated in the excellent Weymouth Museum which used to be housed at Brewers Quay and may well be again by the publication of this book. Its whereabouts since, is a mystery.

If only it could talk.

The King, Charles I, was of course eventually tried and duly executed by order of Parliament, his head being struck from his body at Whitehall on the 30th of January 1649. It is said that he wore two shirts to the scaffold so as not to shiver in front of the assembled crowd who might mistake it for fear. Evidence was found that whilst in captivity, he had actually been negotiating for a Catholic army to invade England on his behalf … Many were of the opinion he had put his subjects through more than enough pain and suffering already.

The King, Charles Stuart, was said to have met his end most courageously though, with the words *"I go now from a corruptible, to an incorruptible crown"*, and, playing the unrepentant martyr to the very end, *"that man of blood"* who believed that he had received his power to rule directly from God, took his final bow.

Eventually, Oliver Cromwell became The Lord Protector of England, spurning the opportunity to be crowned King when it was offered, but, in the end, some would say that he acted almost as shamefully as one. I am not of that opinion. Though, with his final crushing of the Leveller movement at Burford in Oxfordshire, the very men who had been at the forefront of his many victories, he did in the end, show just as much contempt for the ordinary Englishman as any King or Queen had ever done before or after him.

All of the surviving characters from this amazing Dorset saga went their separate ways, most, into the shadowy obscurity that time affords the majority of us, but a few as we shall see on the following pages, went on to make a more indelible mark in that exhilarating and terrible century of rebellion.

Some ordinary soldiers and citizens, perhaps they were dreamers, or even visionaries, hoped that after so many years of bloody civil war, their lot would change for the better and land would be given over to them to work freely. They hoped that after all their sacrifice and hardship they would not simply be exchanging one set of uncaring masters for another. They prayed that this country would never be the same again.

Sadly, they were mistaken.

The Diary of Preacher Peter Ince

The next section is a faithful rendition of a copy, made in 1870, of the diary of Peter Ince, the Puritan preacher of Sydenham's garrison. It is obviously written in the language of the seventeenth century and is therefore, in places, somewhat repetitive. But it does give a fascinating insight into both the extent of the Crabchurch Conspiracy and, of the Parliamentary mindset and response to the carnage that it wrought.

It begins with an almost day by day account of the happenings leading up to and during the Crabchurch Conspiracy and of what life under siege in Melcombe was like during one hard February in the English Civil War.

To my mind, the most startling thing about the diary is the total omission of any mention of the fate of the 250 poor Irishmen who perished in the icy waters of 'The Hole' during the small hours of the Battle of Weymouth.
Of course, we have only the word of the original copier of the diary, that he transcribed it faithfully and in its entirety and, given that he did and would have no other reason to omit the details himself, we are left with something of a puzzle as to why the staunch Puritan Peter Ince saw fit to leave out this very important detail of the story. Colonel William Sydenham himself only makes the briefest mention of it in one of his letters.
It is unlikely that the parliamentarians tried to silence all knowledge of it as they would possibly have seen it as God's justice upon the papists for the atrocities perpetrated against the Protestant settlers in Ireland by Catholics. In one such quite similar incident in Ireland, it was reported that up to three hundred Protestant men, women and children were dispatched in a mass drowning in a river by native Irish Catholics.

Where the handwriting of the original Edwardian transcriber is a little difficult to interpret, I have written what I think the word is most likely to be in italics.
Where a word is totally unintelligible, I have written ***.
I hope that this does not detract in any way from the integrity of the diary, which I have otherwise transcribed in its entirety.

The Diary of Preacher Peter Ince
from Cowdell-Barrett, W.E. (1910)

A brief relation of the surprise of the Forts of Weymouth
The Siege of Melcombe
The Recovery of the Forts
And Raising of the Siege

By P. I. Minister to the Garrison

London. Printed for Luke Parsone at the Parrot in Pauls Church-Yard 1645

Since hath been the goodnesse of God to us, that tis pitty it should passé without a memorial, and record: and the *** that others may not onely blesse God with us, but may be incouraged to a future R*** on the faire power that faced us, if they should fall into the like distresse. To desire not to retract anything from the many acts of divine power and goodnesse, Whereby God hath manifested himself in other places; but certainly there were not since these wars begun, a people more strangely *faced* by the Lord.

In the beginning of February, we were in as sweet a quiet and security as any garrison in the Kingdom: no enemy near us, but one at Portland, and that not very considerable, being but about three or four hundred men – it pleased God, that on a *Suddain*, our Forts and quiet were left, one of the Forts commanded by the harbour, the others the Town. Some of the Townsmen having a long time before hatching a conspiracy with Sir Lewis Dives, and the Portlanders, now brought their *** to execution

On Sabbath day, the ninth of February, about midnight, they did lead our enemies by such secret wayes, that they were upon our sentinels suddenly, and *** and *** the Forts without anything worthy *** resistance; and now a late alarm was given by the drums and the shouts of the Enemies ***ing such dangerous *** possest of two places (which about a half years pain and ***, had made our security) resolved upon a sudden assault, which was attempted, but were repulsed with the losse of the lives of four men, and the blood of more, though not many. Major Sydenham, the Governor's brother(whose memory may not be buried with him) had received a mortall wound, of which he died the day following; his death was no small joy to our enemies, to whom he was a perpetual vexation and terror; and no small grief to us, who had our eyes too much upon him; also Captain Salanova was wounded, and to Melcomb, drew the bridge which lies betwixt the Towns.

This place of Melcomb, our enemies tamely yielded as untenable; and we had scarce bestowed a fortnights work on it since we possest this Garrison, yet

God made it tenable, and so our adversaries found it. All this day they spent their great and small shot lavishly upon us from the Forts, and some of their Gunners ingaged themselves to levell us with the ground; but the weapons forced against us, did not proffer: For our houses stood, and little of our blood was spilt. After they *saw* the multitude , as of great Bullets, and Iron bars, hot and cold, sent against us, did us not the mischief they intended, they abated somewhat of their successlesse ***. Our Horse sallied out some times, and fecht us in some Provisions and ***--

On Tuesday, (11th February 1645) Captain Martin came in the ship called the Providence, from Pool; the sight of any friend was an encouragement, and he was the welcome, because he brought along about four score of our men who were upon and Captain Allen, with some others,

In the morning following, we saw little but *** our own Guns, Powder, Shot, Forts, Gunners, and in a manner, everything but our God, against us. In this condition (when some of our friends defected as lost men, and our enemies look'd upon us conquered) some of us made it a *** of our Belief, That God would be our Saviour, because he had taken other Saviours from us. We had not so much as one ship left us, but what lay under the command of our enemies—

About Noon, Sir Lewis Dives (who was expected sooner, & as some say, should at the same hour, have fallen upon Melcomb) came up with Horse and Foot to ayd the Popish Knight Sir Walter Hastings, in keeping what Villainy and treachery he had gained from us, and to see if they could gain what was yet left us. In the evening we left Weymouth, which we couldn't any longer make good, and fetching our fellows and friends abroad, at the time of the surprise, and might not tell adbvanced by the land passage to us.

On Wednesday (12th February 1645) came the Admirall into the Road, Captain Batten and another of the Parliament's ships, to *** helpfulnesse, both in easing us of our prisoners, of which, we had above 200, and ayding of us with neer 200 men. We must acknowledge ourselves very much indebted. It was a merciful providence of God, that the winds forced at that time to bring them hither.

On Thursday (13th February 1645) our enemies began to fire us; and by small *Iron Skiffs* heated in a forge, which they shot out of their muskets, set fire on a thacht house, *** against the Chappell Fort, from whence they shot about the house continually, to hinder us from quenching the flames, but without the least hurt to any man. This fire was soon put out, it only consumed two houses, blessed be God: Upon this we fell (though unwillingly to the like course, and fired a house in the Chapell Fort; but being little delighted with such sad spectacles, we sent to the enemy that there might be no more such work on either side; the y sent us word, They *** to parley with us, and would do what they pleased –

The day after, (Friday 14th February 1645) they fired again on the other side the Town, over against the North- point Fort, yet that also be quenched without the losse of one drop of blood. Upon this, we fired seven or eight of the Houses in Weymouth; and whiles they endeavoured to rescue their houses from the flames, one was shot dead that betrayed us, and two others were wounded; After this there was no more burning on either side

On Saturday (15th February 1645) came to us our friend, Lieutenant Colonel Haynes, with about 100 horse, which was an addition to our strength ***

The next morning (Sunday 16th February 1645) the Governor (Colonel William Sydenham) (whose valour and unwearied industry we have cause blesse God for) went with Lieutenant Colonell Haynes, and all the horse, and opportunely met with a troop of the enemie's horse (neer Radipole) routed them, took 45 prisoners, about 60 horse, slew 7, or 8 of them ; took a Captain, and a Cornet: And this was donne without the losse of one man, Major Brown, and the Governor's brother (Thomas Sydenham) being only slightly wounded. The Governor and some of our party, chased to whole remnant of them that escaped up to the gates of Weymouth; thereupon, somewhat of the insolency of our enemies was abated, so that we might exchange prisoners, and have a reputation with them

In the beginning of the second week of our trouble, (Monday 17th February 1645) our enemies lying at some further distance than formerly, we had the opportunitie to go abroad with the horse, to fetch in provisions – we brought in 900 sheep, and took a Captain, who expected not to find our *will* so large as we make it, did stumbled upon our men, thinking them to be of his own party.

In both towns there was every day a new expence of shot and blood on both sides; but considering the many advantages they had continually upon us, it did daily cause in us our admiration, that our losses would be so little. Every night we were molested with the loude happinesses, and revilings of our enemies; but the worse we found them, the greater was our hope *** from them.

About the end of this week, came down the Lord Goring from Salisbury, and on the Sabbath-day, all day faced us with his Horse and Foot, No summons came from any of them, whether from a despair of any inclination in us to surrender, or from what other cause it might proceed we know not.

This night they made a work at the north end of the Town, which when the Governor discovered on Monday morning, he resolved to take out a party of foot and horse, and to see if they might be removed to a further distance from us; but before they could be got together, our great shot kil'd some of them, and the rest did not stay; so that we with ease took all their working tools and the work with a few horse; their body of horse standing on a rising ground, not far off, and looking on.

On Tuesday morning (25th February 1645) we went out with our horse and some foot, and met with a party of their horse, going with some provisions to Weymouth; we beat them from their Carriages, brought some of them into Melcomb, and had *** them, had not another party been too near our own Rear, We *** a house at Radipole, a mile from the Town, where we suspected they would *house* some muskettiers , which might have done us small hurt –

Those in Weymouth seeing their horse worsted, and flying before us, *hasted* out a hundred foot for their relief; the Governor being then in the field with the horse, and having intelligence of the motion of their foot out of Weymouth, resolved to fall over the bridge upon the Town, and to attempt the recovery of the Chapel- Fort; which suddenly drawing out severall Squadrons out of *every* Company, he ***- Major Wilson and Captain Langford, led on the party; the enemie not discovering our *mean* till they were upon the out-works, and into the Chappel, and after a shot or two, cried quarter – Thus had we now again regained the command of the Town of Weymouth; took in the Fort and Town above 100 prisoners, one Lieutenant Colonel, one Major, three Captains, besides other officers;

We took about 40 load of provisions of all sorts, which they had brought in the Lords day before; We slew here, their ***, and Philips after, the fourth of the conspirators, who had conspired our ruine, which received his reward; besides three or four other men.

At this time our provisions for horse, were almost exhausted, so that if God had not supplied us out of our enemies store, we had been driven to great extremities –

This invaluable mercy, was the first step to our recovery; Our enemy could not now harbour near us as before, nor relieve their friends in the North-point so easily, being to passé by us; besides, this Fort overlooking Melcomb, did us far more mischief than the North-point. We relieved here some honest men that were their prisoners, which made it more a mercy and took some of the profidious Townsmen, who after taking the Covenant with us, were got into arms against us. *Because* of the pillage in the Town of Weymouth, by both Captain Kaines a papist, his portmantle, where in he had a parcel of Holy Beads, a Commission for a ship to play the Pirate with at sea, which lay blank at Dunkirk, All by Master Henry Jeremius Letters(which we have also) he had his name put in –

Our enemies upon this losse, began to think of packing up, but Sir Lewis was loth to leave us so; and therefore importunes the Lord Goring (who for *ought* we can hear, had no great stomach for the businesse) to try anon-slaught upon us.

On Thursday, they marcht with their Horse, Foot and Carraiges, from Dorchester, towards us; but do so guard all wayes, that no intelligence must come neer us.

Here fell in another strange providence of God for us. One of our men who had been taken prisoner, two or three days before (though very strictly wacht) broke from them, and got safe to our horse there in the field, by him we had notice of all their intendments, where upon we put ourselves into the most prepared posture we could, to secure them. We quit the West-guard of Weymouth, and made a Barricado below in the street beneath the Chappel.Fort, planted a gun there, and ordered all the other guards, so as might serve best for the repulse of them that were coming against us, about one or two of the clock the night (it being light) as they come, The most considerable part of them on the left-side, where *cutting* the work (which we quit) so easily, they thought all their own, and gave a loud hoop, (which ended in heavy groans with some of them not long after) They had not come in a body far down the street, but their presumption was confronted, and they thought themselves further off: A long time shot was going on both sides; but at last seeing they got nothing but wounds, by staying, they began to run away, and be quiet, leaving *** dead men in the streets: One Lieutenant, so wounded, that he could not get off, and some common souldiers, The people saw them carry away some of them Gallants, and since that, they buried some they carried away at Dorchester and other places.

On the other side from the North-point, the Irish Rebels, and others of them *flaternily* fell on, and the Barricado made that way, lying below the houses under the hill, the enemy broke in within the Barricado through the houses, and put our men to a somewhat *** retreat thence; but they fell back to a second Barricado, where a Gun was planted, which they had been in a way to retreat too, but that the Governor came seasonably in, and commanded them to make it good; so they fired the Gun at the enemy, where upon they fled back and were followed by a party, taken off from the main guard, to the further Barricado formerly quitted. Here we wounded another of them that betrayed us, who died of his wound a day or two after. The Governors horse was here shot in the head. Those on the North end of the Town, did onely lie behind a bank. Firing at a distance, and came not up, yet left some of their blood behind *there*. So after about two hours fight, they very silently stole away, that we might not fall upon their Rear. They retreated to Wike, about a mile from the Town, and having stayed a while to use some Chirurgery about their wounds, and to take their friends out of our

Forts along with them; at last they marcht away, cursing and swearing, We were struck with much wonder, to see them leave our Forts, and could not study the meaning of it : But away they went, and left us our Holds and Guns, not past three or four of them spikt; our corn stacks unburnt, our Ships unspoiled, and departed with as little mischief doing, as if they had been our *** friends.

Oh that we could praise the Lord for his goodnesse, and for his wonderfull works, that he doth for the children of ***.And we enjoyed our old quiet, we had not seen so much of God as now we have; and many of us would not for the world have wanted the experiences we have now gained.

We have not lost since our assault upon the Chappel-Fort, any officer, not so much as a Corporall, and not above 20 men; our enemies report their losse of men one way and another, taken, slain, and wounded, 4 or 500, men. Thus God received us without the help of any Army, and Therefore we desire he may have the greater glory.

Since we have been repossessest of our own, we have examined the survivors of them that were *** in the contrivement of our ***; and upon Saturday March the first, Captain Cade, an Alderman of the Town, Thomas Samways a Tailor, John Mils, Walter Bond, are tried by a Conncell of War, and sentenced to be hanged; A fitter reward for their Fact, then the 500 pound, one of them confesses, Sir Lewis was to give them. Cade and Mils and an Irish Rebel, were hanged at the North-point on Monday morning, the other two be repreived to make a further discovery of their partners.

There be not many of the villains left, but their sin hath found them out.

We have found a hope for the discovery of the rest. We hope this place shall be so weeded of such inhabitants, that we shall not *come* *** the like dangers. We desire other places, amongst them, the great Citie of the Kingdom, may learn by us to take heer how they keep false men, and malignant spirits amongst them, who do but wait when they may be employed upon the like Designes.

The God that hath delivered many other places of late, and now us, still *** these mens counsels into __ Foolishnesse, and disappoint the devices of the *Crafty* so that their hands may not bring about their *conspiracies*, We desire our friends may not look upon any valour or activity of ours, as our deliverers; but merely upon what God who gave us whatever courage or successe we had.

To whom, and not to us, be glory forever. Amen.

This concludes the Diary of Preacher Peter Ince.

Confessions of the Crabchurch Conspirators and Witnesses

The following section recorded in 1645, is an account of court records of statements taken from the Crabchurch Conspirators and witnesses to the events leading up to the violence of February 1645 in Weymouth and Melcombe.

(Transcribed from an original 17th century pamphlet in 1870 by an unknown author. It is possible that Peter Ince had a hand in this, but it was in all probability an un-named clerk who painstakingly took down these statements on behalf of Sydenham and Batten)

***

The Last Speeches
and
Confession
of Captain
John Cade and John Mils
Constable

Who were hanged at Waymouth for endeavouring to betray that Garrison to the enemie with all the severall examinations of the Plotters and the sentences denounced against them and others of the said conspiracie

By
W Sydenham, Col. Governor of Waymouth and Captain William Batten, Vice Admirall of the Navie, and the rest of the Counsell of War at Waymouth

With a
Coppie of Sir Lewis Dyves, Letter to Colonell Sydenham about the same, and Colonell Sydenham, his answer.

Imprinted at London by Iane Coe 1645.

I shall first of all present you with an insolent and bould letter sent by Sir Lewis Dives to Colonell Sydenham, as you may perceive by the contents there, directed thus.

For Master Sydenham At Waymouth:

In your last civil letter, which your trumpeter brought to me, you charge me with treachery, and Fabian Hodder and his wife for intelligencers and traitors. Look but upon your own heart, and there you shall find that character clearly written, where with you falsely and injuriously accuse of other men. The desire I had to preserve their innocence from your barbarous inhumanity, was for that I knew their approved loyalty to their sovereign was a crime sufficient to make them expect the worst of ills, from a traitor's hand.

But do your will, and heape vengeance on your own head, by shedding more innocent blood. Paty shall die, deservedly by the law of arms; having quitted the King's service, wherein he was entertained, and turning rebel. And whereas you threaten others of a higher orb shall follow him, know this, that were all my children under the power of your cruelty, I would not be diverted from justice to save their lives. And, for conclusion, be best assured that, if you put to death these innocent persons, I will vindicate this blood to the utmost of that power wherewith God shall enable me, upon you and yours without ever giving quarter to anyone who hath relation to you, which shall faithfully be performed by him that professeth himself your enemy.

Lewis Dyve, Sherborne, the 12th March 1645.

For Sir Lewis Dyve these, at Sherborn Lodge:

You call my last letter 'civil', and yet you seem to be somewhat angry at it; which I should admire, had I not lately given you sufficient cause, for I must confess ingenuously, had I livery and seizon of your castle, I should not be so soon dislodged without some indignation, especially if an army of mine own party (viz Goring's) stood by and looked upon it. You desire me to look upon my own heart; which I have done, and find written there, in the fairest characters, a true desire of advancing God's honour, maintaining the King's just power, and contending for the privileges of the Parliament at Westminster, and the liberty of the subject; which when I find you so maliciously opposing and despitefully stiling treason and rebellion, I am induced to think this age hath produced unparalleled monsters, which are (without slander) 'pestes humani generis' , for traytor I may not call you, which cannot possibly be guilty of such a sin in the opinion of 'Aulicus' the only author which (it seems by your language) you are versed in.

You are very tender of shedding innocent blood, and therefore Paty must die; but good Sir Lewis, for what crime? He served, you say, on your side; I have heard 'tis (as you do) only as a scribe; and hath since turned rebel, because he would not tamely stand still whiles you were plundering him.

'Heu nefas infandum'! for this, right or wrong, the poor man must suffer, (and setting honesty aside) you will be just for certain.

May it please your worship to be merciful too, if not to him, yet to me and mine (when we fall into your hands); till when your last experience might remember you that I am as far from fearing, as my present condition is far from needing your quarter, which I hope I shall have an opportunity to dispute further of with you; whom to any man in England, I shall answer in this quarrel. In the mean, know that I intend to make a halter of your letter to hang Hodder with; whose crime is the first contrivance of that treachery, which you after (tho, blessed be God! but simply) acted to the losse of what you valued worth a crowne.

Paty you may hang, but will not be able to bury; which may occasion a great mortality amongst you. And therefor be advised to forebear, by him, to whom proclaiming yourself a professed enemy, you have invited me as professedly to subscribe myself.

Yours W Sydenham.

Weymouth and Melcombe Regis
At a Council of War there held the first day of March 1644 before the Governor, and all the Field officers and Captains of the Garrison of Weymouth and Melcomb Regis and also before Captain William Batten, Vice Admirall of the Navy, and Admirall of the Fleet then riding in Weymouth, and divers other Sea Captains then present.

Walter Bond of Waymouth on his own voluntarie oath affirmeth that Thomas Samwaies of this towne Jaylor, on Sunday last fortnight about eight of the clocke at night, in the house of William Philips, since deceased, in the presence of John Seton, Jo Dry Tanner, the said William Philips, Leonard Symonds since dead Walter Mich & Jo Mills, Constable, Samuell Takle Baker, and John Lock say, that on that night following he would have the doores of the Marshallsay broken up and that Portland men would come in and helpe, and that the gates of the towne would be opened unto them ; and this Examinant saith, that all the persons before named, were in the house before he came in, and that he this Examinant stayed not there above a quarter of an houre, and went thence a Shipboard, and there stayed till about one of the clocke, and then came home, and was going to bed, at which time, Robert Bun, and Edward Dove, both of Portland, came to this Examinants house in Waymouth & caused him to go up to the North point saying, that it was taken for King Charles; And this examinant went thither with the said Bun and Doby, and did service there in the north point and helpt loaded the ordnance; and this examinant saith that Humpherie Tolier and he this Examinant both knew that the North point was taken, and this Examinant saith, that the said John Dry said, at the same time, that he was to go to the passage to helpe on the Portland men, and then spake to the said Mils to go with him, to which he made no reply but smiled at it.

Thomas Samwaies of this towne Tailor, on his voluntarie oath saith, that Fabian Hodder about a moneth sithence, at the prison told this Examinant. That Sir lewis Dives would gather his forces together and would come and surprise this Towne with the help of Portland men; And saith he, this Examinant after met with Captain John Cade, at Fabian Hodders house in the presence of Hodders wife told this Examinant, that on Sabbath day last this fortnight, Sir lewis Dives and the Portland Forces would come and surprise this Towne, and willed him to tell Walter Bond, Mariner, William Philips and Leonard Symonds, of the time of the surprise. And this Examinant told the said Bond of it accordingly, unto which Bond said, that he would be with his ship in the Hole, and that if Portland men came, he would be ready to assist them in getting into the North Fort; And this Examinant saith, That none was present but himself when he delivered the message to Bond. This examinant further saith, That the said Cap Cade on Tuesday or Wednesday morning, after the Forts were surprised by the enemy, met this Examinant at his door, spake to him, this Examinant, to this purpose, viz. Come let us get a Company, and sieze upon the Main Guard, and let down the Bridge, and let over the Kings Forces, and sieze on, and break open the prison door.

John Mills of Waymouth, Constable, consefesseth, That on Sunday last was fortnight, he, this Examinant, about six of the clock at night, was in the house of the said William Philips, to look for Thomas Alexander, where were present, Walter Bond, Thomas Samwayes, John Dry, William Philips, and Thomas Alexander and saith, That he spake to no body there, nor any to him, and stayed there not half a quarter of an hour, and went thence to Thomas Alexander and there slept and being charged, that the morning when this Town was surprised, that he had a handkerchief about his arm in the streets, denieth it. He had a handkerchief on his arm in the house.

The said Thomas samwayes, further voluntarily deposeth, That about a week before the Forts of this garrison were surprised, Fabian Hodder composed an oath in writing to this effect, viz. You shall swear by the Holy Trinity, that you will conceal the intended Plot; which oath, Fabian Hodder's wife brought to this examinant, and told him, that all that were made acquainted with the Plot, Should take the said oath; And further this Examinant saith, that Captain Cade told this Examinant, That before he discovered the said Plot to any, they should take the said oath.

Captain Richard Yeardly on his voluntary oath, affirmeth, That on the Monday morning when the Forts of this Town were surprised, he saw John Mills, one of the Constables of this Town, with an handkerchief knit about his Arm, which was reported to be a signe used by Portland men when they came to surprise the Forts.

William Mineterne of this Town mariner, on his voluntary oath said, That about a weeke before the Forts were surprised, Captain John Cade meeting with this Examinant between Radipole and this towne, The said Captaine cade said to this Examinant, that there were forces were coming to take this town of Waymouth and Melcombe Regis, and asked of this Examinant, whether hee would be one of those that would assist in keep gaining of the Town, and desired him to put his hand to a list in writing to that purpose, to be of the Company for betraying of the Town and further saith, that the said Captain awers other times after solicited this Examinant to further the designe upon the Town.

The Examination of Anne the wife of Fabian Hodder of this Towne Merchant: 3 March 1644.

Who saith that shee, this Examinants husband about Christmas last, had writ to Sir lewis Dive at Sherborn, to this effect. That Portland men would come, and take the Forts of this Town, if the said Sir Lewis Dive would please to come, and take the Towne of Melcombe, which letters was unsealed and delivered by this Examinant to Elizabeth Wall widow, daughter of mistris Thomazine Dennis Widow, with the contents of which Letters, this Examinant acquainted the said Elizabeth Wall, who undertook to convey the same Letters to Sir Lewis Dive. To which Letters Sir Lewis Dive made answer in writing (which was sent to this Examinants husband by the said Elizabeth Wall) that he would come up with 1500 Horse and Foot, on Sabbath last was three weeks, about midnight, which was neare about the time that the Forts were surprised by Portland men. And this Examinant further saith, that her husband about a week before the Forts were surprised, wrote another letter to Sir Lewis Dive to the like effect as the former, which this Examinant delivered to Thomas Samwaies Taylor, to be conveyed by the said Elizabeth Wall, which said Elizabeth did often come to this Examinants house, in messages from Richard Mighill, and another Gunner sithence killed, who were put out of this Town and afterwards lived in Portland. And this Examinant saith, that on Saturday last was three weekes, which was the day before the execution of the designe, the Governor of Portland and others there sent to this examinants husband in writing, that they would come in the next day; which Letters was brought by the said Elizabeth Wall to this Examinant, and delivered by her husband.

March 10th 1645

John Barnes of Preston husbandman affirmeth, that John Anthony, and Edward Flatman, on Thursday last, said that Robert Bowyer, John Bowyer, Andrew Galshell, Thomas Galchell and the said Edward Flatman, and divers others to the number of thirtie and upwards, knew of the intention of the late surprisal of the forts of this Garrison, before they were surprised by the Cavaliers. And knew that the word was Crabchurch and the signe was a white handkercheife about their Armes

March 11th 1645

The said Robert Boyer being examined saith that about six weeks sithence, one of the soldiers in arms for the Parliament, left a musket at this Examinant's house, which being demanded by the Forces in Armes against the Parliament, that lately came to this Garrison, this Examinant told them he would serve in the sad musket himself, to this intent (as this Examinant saith) to preserve the same musket. And accordingly this Examinant took his musket and marched with the Cavaliers unto Causeway, about a day or two after the Forts of this Garrison were surprised by the Enemy, where this Examinant stayed about one houre, and half, and then in the evening returned unto his house in Sutton with his musket, and there staid and went abroad no more afterwards. And this Examinant saith, that he had some match and powder, but no bullets, Bandoleers, or sword, and that hee did not charge his musket. And further this Examinant saith, that Master Wood Clerk Curate of Sutton, John Fieldew, Edward Flatman, and Thomas Galshell were all at Causeway in the company of the Cavaliers. And afterwards they returned unto Sutton aforesaid, but whether any of them had Armes or no, this Examinant knoweth not, for that, As this Examinant saith, he was distempered with beere, And this Examinant saith, that he was not enlisted in any Company, or under any command, And that on his march towards Causeway, he discharged his musket, which was loaden with Powder only, once or twice.

The said John Bowyer being examined saith that on Sunday, when the Forts of this Garrison were surprised about halfe an hour after sun setting, William Wilsheer of Sutton aforesaid, came to this Examinant's house, and asked this Examinant, whether he would goe forth in the fields and see if the King's army was coming, upon which the Examinant, and said Wilsheere, went into Sutton Cowleaze called Jordan, and there met with those named in the margent of this Examinant's examination,

Edward Flatman
John Fieldew
Will Willsheer
Tho Cox
John Meech Junior
Alexander Butcher
John Aeir
And two of Upway

John Bowyer
John Bryer

who had no Armes save that Master Fieldew had a Pistoll. And this Examinant saith, that all the same parties met in that place to meet the Kings Army, that were coming against the Town of Waymouth and Melcomb Regis And stayed about an hour and more and thence went unto Week Oliver and safe there about an hour and drank a pipe of Tabbacco and went thence to the higher end of W Kain's Ground in the Cowleaze & stayed there a houre; and thence came to Aewhouse Master Kaines Dayrie house, and there a little above that house stayed about an houre to see the coming of the Kings Army, and there saw shooting against the town, and did conceive the Town taken by the KingsArmy, and said before they conceived the Kings Army would not come down to take the Town

The said Andrew Galshell alias Blanchard being examined saith, that on Sunday night, before the Forts of this Garrison were surprised, John Fieldew came to this Examinant, at his house about two houres in the night, and told him that the kings forces were coming down to take this Town, and told this Examinant that he had gotten some Company, and spake to the Examinant to go with him that night, saying that it would be worth to him five pounds, but this Examinant refused to go with him, and went to bed.

The said Thomas Galshell, alias Blanchard being examined saith, that on Sunday night before the Forts of this town were surprised, John Fieldew about two hours in night came to this Examinant, and spake to him to go with him that night, and promised him that it would be worth to him five pounds, but this Examinant saith that he refused to goe with him and went to bed, and further saith that the Wednesday following hee this Examinant, and Roger Bowyer, Simon Wilsheere, John Wood Clerke, John Feildue, and Edward Flatman, went to Caseway to see the Souldiers, because they were reported to be a great Army: And saith that this Examinant and the said Robert Bowyer, and William Wilsheere, stayed at Causeway at the Ale house about two houres, and then returned unto Sutton

The said John Bryer being examined saith, That John Feildue came to him that Sunday night, before the Forts of this Town were surprised, and spake to him to go with him a mile or two that night, And this Examinant saith, that about an hour or two in night, that Sunday night, John Feildue, John Bowyer, John Meech the younger, William Wilsheere, Edw Flatman, Thomas Coxe, Alexander Butcher, John Aeur, and six or seven of Upway and Broadway, whose names this Examinant doth not know, met all in Radipoll Field, about M Kaynes Dairie House; And saith that they all staid there in that place, about three or four houres, until about an hour after the beginning of the onset on this Town by Portland men. And this Examinant saith, that during the fight, M Feildue told the company, that he conceived that Portland men had entered the Aore; and saith; That the said John Feildue, the same Sunday after evening prayer, at the widdow Bradfords house, none being present but the said John Feildue and the said Examinant, that this Town would be taken that night; And further saith, That the said John Feildue by the way as they went into Radipoll field, and in the field when they met all together, told them that the designe was that Portland men were that night were to surprise the North point, and Sir Lewis Dive with his Forces were to make an onset on Melcomb, with the assistance of the said Feildue and the rest of the said Companie; and staid that they all said in Radipoll field about two hours after the onset by Portland men, expecting Sir Lewis Dives forces, and they were not coming all of them returned unto Sutton and their own homes; And saith, the Upway men had long staves, and one of them a Welch hook and Mr Feildue a pistol, and all the rest but sticks in their hands; And that the number of the persons so met together, were in all about sixteen and saith that Mr Feildue told all the said Companie, that the word was Crabchurch, and further saith, that the said John Meech the younger, came down to this town to fetch the word, but what word, this Examinant knoweth not

The said William Wilsheere being examined saith, that John Feildue on Sunday in the evening, before the Forts were surprised, sent Alexander Bencher to this Examinamt, to have him come to the said Feildue which he did accordingly, And then the said feildue spake to this Examinant, to go with him to Week Oliver, And there met with the said John Feildue, John Bryer, Alexander Butcher, Edward Flatman, John Meech the younger, , John Bowyer and Thomas Coxe, and there stayed about half an hour after this Examinamt coming thither, and went thence to Radipoll, by Mr kaynes Dairie house, and there met with Richard Keale and John Hayne of Broadway or Upway; And saith, that Mr Fieldue and the said Meech had Pistols, Haine, a Welch hook, and the rest Cudgels; And saith that John Meech told this Examinant, that if the Town were taken they should have five l a piece, and said that the Cavaliers word was Crabchurch. And the said Meech told this Examinant, that he had both words from the Town, and then Mr Feildue told this Examinant and the rest of the Companie that Portland men would surprise the North Fort, and that Sir Lewis Dive would come with his forces, and make an onset on Melcomb, and in expectation of the coming of his Forces, this Examinant and the rest stayed about an hour and half after the onset by the Portland men, and then returned to their own homes.

The confession of Nicholas Chappell, taken the 17th of Febr 1645
That John Mills on Friday February 7. went out of Portland, to Fleet, and came back on Saturday night, and on Sunday Febr 9. order was given at Portland Church, that all Islanders and Souldiers should appear at the Castle

by five of the clocke, with their Arms, And a partie was chosen and sent along the Beach, whom John Dry a Tanner met at the passage, and conducted them to the Chappell Fort: A partie was sent by Water, whom Walter Bond a Fisherman of Hope met at the Peere, and conducted them to the North Point: And the said Nicholas Chappell heard the Enemie say, the Gunners were consenting to the Plot, and that John Feildue was to come on Melcomb side with 60 men, and to be let into the Town, but by whom this Examinant knoweth not; And that the number of men brought over for the surprisall of the Forts were 120. with whom the Townesmen were to joyn.

There is already condemned by the Councell of War, Walter Bond a Sailer, Thomas Samways a Tayler, that dwelt in Melcomb, John Mills the Constable of the Town, and Captain John Cade; besides an Irish Rebell a native Papist, that put a rope about his own neck and hanged himself

1.Captain John Cade is hanged, according to sentence denounced against him by the Councell of War, whose confessions is before amongst the Examinations: Besides which, he made no other at all; for when he was upon the ladder, all that he would say before he died was onely this, that he could say no more than he had said already, and so died

2 John Mills the Constable is also hanged according to sentence denounced against him by the Councell of War, who died most desperately; what he said at his Examination is before, since which nothing more would be compelled by him, nor any signe or token of sorrow or repentance, But when he was upon the Ladder, he most desperately threw himself off, not showing any signes of humiliation or calling upon God for mercie on his soul, but carelessly in a most desperate manner died, not so much as praying to God to receive his soul

3 Walter Bond Sailer, he was reprieved by the Councell of War, and is now in the prison, his confession is before.

4 Thomas Samways the Tayler that lived in Melcomb, he was reprieved by the Counsell of Warre, and hath expressed much Sorrow for his treacherous fact; He was brought to the Gallowes to be hanged, but upon his penitency and confession he was reprieved and carried back to the prison

5 The irish Rebell hanged himself without judgement or execution doing all upon himself

6 Divers of them are slain; Fabian Hodder and others, are in Prison at Poole, and other places, not yet tried, and some are run away.

Finis

A Condensed Biography of the Principal Characters from the Crabchurch Conspiracy

The Gentlemen of the Army of Parliament

<u>Colonel William Sydenham</u>:

Sadly, I can find no original portrait of William Sydenham. His religious leanings were described as Presbyterian Independent. In 1645 he was Governor of the twin towns of Weymouth & Melcombe and also elected as M.P for Melcombe. In 1648, Parliament ordered that William Sydenham be paid a thousand pounds as recompense for his arrears of pay during his military service in their cause, this money to be raised from *"discoveries of delinquents land"*. In other words, the money came from either the selling off of or the use of the sequestered lands of defeated royalists.

On the 14th August 1649 he, along with Colonel Fleetwood, became joint Governor of the Isle of Wight, and with this appointment came the task of caring for the late King's children for a time.

In 1653, William's ascendancy to political power really began with Cromwell's expulsion of the Long Parliament which had first been set up by King Charles on the 3rd November 1640. This was replaced by the Rump Parliament and on the 29th April 1653 William Sydenham was elected by the officers of the New Model Army as one of the thirteen members of it. However, his views were somewhat conservative for the Rump and many arguments ensued. On the 12th December 1653, he led the way in proposing that the Rump Parliament dissolve itself, thereby setting himself up as one of the leading founders of Cromwell's Protectorate.

In 1654 Cromwell repaid his loyalty by appointing him as one of the Commissioners of the Treasury. And along with his other duties, this gave William an annual income of two thousand pounds a year; a vast amount at that time.

He sat for Dorset in the Parliaments of 1654 and 1656 and distinguished himself in debates as a very shrewd and passionate politician. One particular incident of note is where he defended an ex roundhead soldier, turned Quaker preacher, called James Naylor (one of the 'valiant sixty') who was accused of blasphemy because he dared re-enact Christ's entry into Jerusalem by entering the city of Bristol on a donkey ! William spoke up in parliament for the man with these words. *"We live as parliament men but for a time, but we live as Englishmen always. I would not have us be so tender of the privilege of parliament as to forget the liberties of Englishmen".* Words that many present day politicians would do well to heed and act upon.

In 1657, William was summoned to appear in The House of Lords and a Republican pamphlet of the time wrote of him, *"he hath not been thorough-paced for tyranny in time of parliaments",* it was hoped he might yet be *"so redeemed as never to halt or stand off for the future against the Protector's interest"*

Following Cromwell's death on the 3rd September 1658, his surviving son, the indecisive Richard Cromwell took over as Lord Protector of England and William Sydenham became a member of his ruling council. But the 'new Cromwell' was no Oliver and soon it became clear to all that he just wasn't man enough for the job in hand. His mocking nickname at the time was 'Tumbledown Dick' and in April 1659, Sydenham, along with two other prominent parliamentarians, Fleetwood and Desborough, forced Richard Cromwell to dissolve the 3rd Protectorate Parliament in what became known as the 'Wallingford House Party'.

Due to the unbounded generosity of a good friend from the southern states of America, Katie Brown-Gurley, I am most fortunate in owning a wonderful little letter from this period which is signed by William Sydenham and also by another very prominent figure of the Protectorate, the lawyer, Bulstrode Whitelocke. Though it has nothing to do with the above episode, it is still an enigmatic reminder of when the son of a Dorset Squire, held sway over all of England at her most perilous hour.

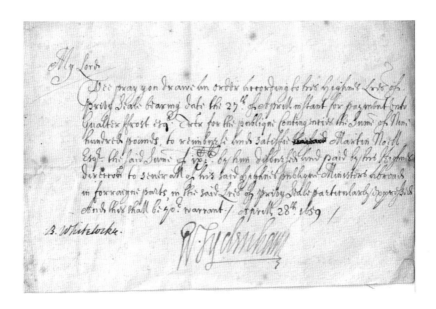

As best I can make out, the letter reads:

My Lord
Wee pray you drawe an order according to his highness Lord of Privy
Seale bearing date the 27th of Aprill instant for payment unto Gualter
Frost esq. [T]-ter for the p-bli[gu]e [C]onting [int]i[s] the summe of
Nine hundred pounds to reimburse and satisfie Martin North esqr the
said summe of IX C L by him disbursed and paid by his highness d—
eccon (discretion ?) to severall of his said highness public[q](ue) Ministers
abroad in forraigne parts, [in] the said Lord of Privy Seale particularly
expressed. And this shall be yo(ur) warrant Aprill 29th 1659
B Whitelocke
W Sydenham

Richard Cromwell was sidelined and The Rump Parliament was restored, with William becoming a member of the Committee of Safety on 7th May and a week or so later, he was also made a member of the Council of State. He was then given command of a regiment of foot. But when Colonel John Lambert 'turned out the Rump Parliament' by use of force, Sydenham played a full part and had to answer to the Council of State as to his conduct in this violent episode. He attested that they were *"necessitated to make use of this last remedy by a particular call of divine providence".*

The Rump Parliament was restored and, not happy   with Sydenham's excuses, he was expelled from it on the 17th January 1660 and his regiment taken from him.

Later in 1660, at the Restoration of the late King's son Charles 11 to the English throne, William was included on the 'Act of Indemnity and Oblivion' as one of the eighteen most dangerous men in the Kingdom. This meant that he was permanently banned from ever again holding any public office and also had to enter into a bond to *"not disturb the peace of the Kingdom"*, but by this time his health was failing.

He died, at home in Wynford Eagle manor in July1661 at the age of just 46, nursed to the end by his devoted younger brother and comrade in arms, Doctor Thomas Sydenham, William's wife, Grace, dying just one week after her husband. Their eldest daughter, Mary (named after William's brave-heart mother) eventually married the painter, Sir James Thornhill. (the first ever painter to be knighted)

 A contemporary wrote of William:

> *"He was one of the most brilliant men of the day and had a paramount influence in the councils of the Parliaments only second to that of Oliver Cromwell".*

> And later: *"Such are the vagaries of time, that the military and political exploits of William, the eldest son, which brought him both fame and notoriety in his lifetime, are now completely forgotten".*

His son, also named William, inherited the estate and house, but heaped shame and dishonour upon the proud family name. A compulsive gambler, he owed so much money that in 1709 he decided to put the house and the estate up as a lottery prize to enable himself to pay his many debtors. What the numerous purchasers of the tickets were unaware of though was that 'young William' had fixed the draw so that a distant cousin of his won the prize. She had secretly agreed with him, that for a suitable financial consideration, she would then hand the house and land back to him so that he could continue as before. The lottery made an immense amount of money and the Grand Draw was made in London. She duly won the star prize of course but, the next part of his scheme did not quite go according to plan. The cousin instead, gave him notice to quit, saying that she now intended to live at Wynford Eagle Manor with her new husband, Doily Mitchell, Esquire. The outraged Sydenham refused to vacate the family pile and together with his two daughters was forcibly evicted and thrown into Dorchester jail. He died there in 1718, a penniless vagrant.

I can now reveal that I have discovered that the author of the famous Dorset smuggling novel entitled Moonfleet, J Meade Falkner, used Colonel William Sydenham as a template for his character, Blackbeard's Ghost. There are far too many coincidences for this not to be so.

In the novel, Blackbeard who is represented as a ghostly figure who stalks the village of Moonfleet at night, was a Colonel in the Parliamentary army, who was once Governor of Carisbrooke Castle on the Isle of Wight, just as William Sydenham was. Furthermore, the young hero of the novel is called John Trenchard. Sydenham's father in law was called Sir John Trenchard. And the heroine of the novel is called Grace. Sir John Trenchard had a daughter called Grace who became Colonel William Sydenham's wife.

It would appear to me that J Meade Falkner was well acquainted with the Crabchurch story and could it just be that although there is now no known portrait of Colonel William Sydenham, Falkner once gazed upon one and took the features of this forgotten Dorset hero and bestowed them upon the character of Blackbeard's ghost ? It is, in the end, only supposition on my part of course, but it all seems to fit perfectly and, could we further surmise that there was indeed a lost diamond from Carisbrooke Castle as in the novel, which was once owned by the King or one of his children who were quartered there and, which somehow found its way into the possession of Colonel William Sydenham of Wynford Eagle in Dorset ?

We shall probably never know, but it is one more possible twist to this already enthralling tale of Dorset during the English Civil Wars.

***

Doctor Thomas Sydenham:

Picture from The College of Physicians of Philidelphia (www.historyofvaccines.org/ content)

Born on the 10th September 1624, he served as a Cornet in his older brother; Francis's dragoon troop and fought in the Battle of Weymouth. He eventually went on to become a Captain of Horse in Colonels Rich's Regiment. Whilst on active service in Essex, he was, for some reason one night, accosted in his quarters by a drunken soldier who grabbed him and aimed a pistol at his chest, intent on murdering him. The man pulled the trigger, but the piece misfired and he succeeded only in *'shattering his own hand'*. Thomas was also numbered among the dead on one battlefield, but was later found to be alive and eventually recovered.

This was to the very great fortune of the English medical profession, as after the wars, Thomas resumed his medical studies at Oxford and became a Doctor. He made such a name for himself in that field that he became known as *"The English Hippocrates"*. A fellow physician, John Brown wrote of him, *"He is the Prince of practical medicine, whose character is as beautiful and as genuinely English as his name"*.

Thomas Sydenham believed that nature had a cure for all of man's ailments and that physicians were merely nature's assistants. One of his few recorded quotes was *"Of all the remedies it has pleased almighty God to give man to relieve his suffering; none is so universal and so efficacious as opium."*

Among his many achievements was the discovery and identification of a disease which became known as 'Sydenham's Chorea". We know it today as St Vitus Dance. In 1659, he was nominated for Parliament, but not elected.

There appears to be no record of Thomas and Dr. Richard Wiseman having ever met, though they almost certainly would have, as both practised in London after the war. And what a strange irony it is, that the two most eminent physicians of the entire seventeenth century, once opposed each other under arms for two weeks, across a few yards of icy seawater in Dorset.

A memorial to Dr Thomas Sydenham, which was erected in the 19th century by the now defunct 'Sydenham Society', can be found halfway up a staircase in St James Church, Pall Mall. The staff there being completely unaware of who this great Dorset man of medicine was.

After a brilliant career, he died of gout, aged 65, at his home in Pall Mall, on the 29th December 1689. He is buried in St James Churchyard, Piccadilly.

***

Major Francis Sydenham:

No known original portrait of Francis Sydenham exists. He left a will dated September 4th 1644 just weeks after the murder of his mother. It simply read; *"I bequeath all of my goods to my father in trust for my wife and children"*. The Parliament only ever paid his wife Mary £80 for her loss, a paltry sum for the many heroic services which her husband rendered to the 'good old cause' during his relatively brief, but very impressive military service. Hopefully his body found its way home to Wynford Eagle and a decent burial. This great and unsung son of Dorset deserved nothing less.

***

Of the two remaining Sydenham brothers, John and Richard, it is John who seems to have been most inspired by his older sibling's example. Born on the 26th February 1627, he was probably not involved in the fighting at Weymouth. But later in the wars, he did see military service in Ireland with Colonel Stubbes Regiment. He was then transferred to Cromwell's Scottish campaign and as a Major, may well have been for a short time, the Governor of Stirling Castle. He was killed in a skirmish just prior to the Battle of Dunbar in May 1651, aged just 24 years. He was known by many as 'The Puritan Major'.

Richard, the youngest sibling, was a Captain but did not apparently see action. Instead he became a civil servant, responsible for raising funds to keep the army in the field. He too died at the age of 24, his cause of death is not recorded in my sources.

***

Preacher Peter Ince:

The diarist preacher who left us such an interesting account of what occurred in the twin towns during that bloody and terrifying month, stayed in Melcombe until February 1647, when on the 26th day of that month, almost two years to the day since the Battle of Weymouth, he took over the ministry of Donhead St Mary in Wiltshire. There he stayed until 1662, when, as one of the almost 2000 victims of a political/religious phenomenon known as The Great Rejection, he was dispossessed of this parish and had to instead, seek employment as a shepherd on the estate of a Mr Grove.

With the return of the House of Stuart to the throne of England, many social changes occurred in religious and general life and this was obviously done as a means of purging all those of the Puritan persuasion, most of who would have sided with the Parliamentry cause during the civil wars. The 'Great Rejection' came about as a result of the Act of Uniformity which required all Church of England Ministers to conform to the Book of Common Prayer by no later than St Bartholomew's Day or lose their position. Those who lost their ministries thereafter preferred to call it 'Black Bartholomew's Day, after a massacre on that date in 1572.

It so happened that the wife of the aforementioned Mr Grove, was suddenly taken very ill and her husband, fearing the worst, sent for the Parish Minister to attend her and pray with her. But this man refused to come straight away as he was about to go hunting and this so enraged Mr Grove that he flew into a foul temper. One of his servants though suddenly had an idea and spoke up. *"Sir, our shepherd, if you will send for him, can pray, very well; we have often heard him at prayer in the field."* And so, the 'Puritan Shepherd', Peter Ince, former Minister to the Parliamentary Garrison of Weymouth and Melcombe, was summoned to attend this ailing rich woman in her most dire hour of need.

Mr Grove looked the Shepherd up and down and asked him if he had ever prayed. Ince stared back, unflinching and replied, *"God forbid, sir, I should live one day without prayer."* With that Grove bade him pray for his wife and, after Ince was done, Grove and those members of his family there present, rose from their knees, somewhat astonished at Ince's skills that he immediately said *"Your language and manner discover you to be a very different person from what your present appearance indicates. I conjure you to inform me who and what you are, and what were your views and situation in life before you came into my service."* With that, Ince admitted to his past and Grove was so impressed that he proclaimed, *"Then you shall be my shepherd"* and built Ince a meeting house on his estate in which he gradually built up a congregation of Dissenters and became known as "Preaching Ince".

***

Lieutenant Colonel James Heane (Haynes):

A distinguished soldier, he eventually took over as commanding officer of Sydenham's old regiment and also as Governor of Melcombe. Charles II, a fugitive after the defeat of his army at the Battle of Worcester in 1651, attempted to find shelter for the night at Bridport, a small Dorset market town twenty miles west of Weymouth, famed for supplying the 'Bridport Dagger', or, hangman's rope. Charles 11 wrote that he and his companions found the town to be *"full of red-coated soldiers"*. These were definitely Heane's troops, who were of course by then a part of the red coated New Model Army, and they were known to be in Bridport on that particular night, prior to marching to Weymouth. At Weymouth they embarked upon a voyage to Jersey with the sole objective of bringing about the capitulation of the very last Royalist stronghold in Britain.

The Cavalier commander on that Channel Island was the 'resourceful' Sir George de Carteret, who held out for several weeks, even dabbling in piracy to boost his coffers. Finally, with the arrival of a huge mortar from Portsmouth, the Roundheads were at last able to end the siege of his stronghold in Elizabeth Castle, where de Carteret had made his base. One shot from the monster weapon went straight through the roof of the family chapel, carried on through the floor and on in to the garrison's arsenal below. With that, Sir George knew that his time was up and immediately discussed terms for surrender. That done he cordially invited Heane and his fellow Parliamentarian officers to a banquet which was to be held on the night before he was due to hand over tenure of his castle to them.

However, de Carteret, a stickler for etiquette, would not allow any of the enemy to enter his fortress until the agreed and appointed hour for surrender had arrived on the following morning. So instead, he had his servants set up a full banquet table, complete with the best silver and candelabras, on the rocks that surrounded the castle.

De Carteret, Heane and their fellow guests ate their meal by moonlight as the waves lapped about their rocky perch!

Sadly, James Heane was killed in a duel in the Caribbean a few years later.

***

The Gentlemen of the King's Army

Doctor Richard Wiseman:

Picture from The History of Surgery and Anaesthesia (www.historyofsurgery.co.uk)

Born in 1621, he qualified as a doctor just before the outbreak of the English Civil War, which meant that his sterling service at the Siege and Battle of Weymouth was done at the tender age of just twenty-three.

He was captured at the Battle of Worcester on 3rd September 1651 and imprisoned for several weeks. Released in 1652, he was again arrested in 1654 for plotting the escape of a prominent royalist from the Tower of London, but the evidence against him was somewhat weak and he was once again released. In 1657, he joined the Spanish Navy and served there for three years, finally returning to England in 1660 at the Restoration of the Monarchy.

He eventually became the principal surgeon and friend to King Charles II and Master of the Barber Surgeons. He married Mary, a grand-daughter of Sir Thomas Mauleverer, the regicide (one of the signatories of the death warrant of Charles I). An avid writer of his experiences and, the author of books on medicine, his most famous work was Severall Chirurgicall Treatises and in it, his wonderfully descriptive pen was as good as ever it was when describing his experiences in Weymouth, as the following text will confirm.

"A gentleman of about sixty years of age, labouring of a hydrocele, was referred to me by Dr Morrison. The swelling was within the tunicles of

the right testicle, the scrotum was thick. I let out the water by puncture with a cannula; it was drained a quart: then I dressed it., and on the third day applied a restrictive emplaster over it with a truss. He was cured in a few days and discharged.

This staunch Royalist died in 1676 and is buried in Covent Garden.

***

Fabian Hodder:

Almost nothing is known of what the chief architect of the Crabchurch Conspiracy did in the years after his timely escape from Poole jail. But back in the twin towns, he was not forgotten by the inhabitants, as is recorded in 1646 by mariner, John Bure (or Bower)

He states to a court that on *"Wednesday last, about seven o'clock in the evening"*, he being on the quay near the George, heard John Jourdain say to Mr. Henry Rose, one of the bailiffs and justices of the town, that *"he was a Cavalier and as bad as Fabian Hodder or worse, and a two faced knave"*. Rose was said to have replied that he would *"throw down all again"*. David Dove, a gunner of the Garrison then heard Jourdain reply to Rose, *"Thou art a double faced man and Fabian Hodder is an honester man than thou"*.

Hodder, next re-enters the written record on his own behalf at the time of the Restoration where he is mentioned as living back in Melcombe, having been restored as an Alderman on the 13th October 1662 and was for a time, also Captain at Portland Castle.

This is the final Will of Fabian Hodder, the arch Conspirator. It is interesting to note that this staunch royalist counts the years of the reign of Charles 11 from January 1649, the year that Charles 1 was executed and not 1660 when Charles 11 was set upon the throne of England:

In the name of God Amen I
Fabian Hodder of Weymouth and Melcombe Regis in the county of Dorset merchant
the twentieth day of September in the thirtie third yeare of the reigne of Our Soveriegne Lord Charles the Second by the Grace of God of all England Scotland France and Ireland King Defender of the Faith ? and in the yeare of Our Lord One thousand six hundred eightie and one being of perfect memorie and remembrance praised be God doe make and ordaine this my last will and testament ? and forme following (viz) First I bequeath my soul into the hands of Almightie God my Maker hoping that through the mercy ? and passion of Jesus Christ my only Saviour and Redeemer to receave ?all pardon and foregiveness of all my synns and as for my bodie to be buried in Christian Buriall at the direction of my executrix hereafter in? nominated in the Church within the towne of Melcomb Regis as neare to my former wife Ann as shall be convenient Item whereof my former wife Ann of late deceased did in her lifetime give unto several relations and friends as she thought fitt I the said Fabian Hodder doe ratifie allow and confirme what my said wife Ann did soe doe and I doe freely give and bequeath and my desire is that such friends and relations shall have such summes of money and other goods and chattels as my said wife Ann did give in her lifetime and by her paper ? to that purpose may appeare, Item I doe also give and bequeath to everyone of those friends and relations that my former wife Anne gave to (as by her paper may appear) as much in value to each of them as my said wife gave to each of them, to be payd in lawfull English money Item I doe give to my Sonn in Law Richard Hodder the summe of five pounds of lawfull money of England Item all the rest of my Goods chattels implements of household Leases Lands and Tenements whatsoever I doe hearby freely give and bequeathe unto my now loving wife Mary her heires and assignes forever, upon Condition that shee shall pay all my debts and bequests and make her sole Executrix of this my last Will and Testament revoking all Other wills and testaments by mee formerly made In witness whereof I the said Fabian Hodder have hereunto put my hand and seale the day and yeare first above written Fabyan Hodder Sealed signed and published in the presence of Elizabeth Lacortnce the marke of Mary Roberts. Geor. Vincent.

Probatum fuit testamentum suprascriptum apud London
Venerabili et   viro domino
*   Magistro custode fuit*
commissario legit? Constituto vicesimo quarto die mensis Novembris Ano
Domini millesimo sexcentesimo Octogesimo primo (24th *November*
1681)juramanto Maria Hodder
Reliectie et executrices in ? testamento

Williams, S (2012)

***

George, Lord Goring;

After the humiliation of the Battle of Weymouth, Goring marched off to besiege Taunton in Somerset, but never quite succeeded in taking it. He was finally brought to battle by the legendary Roundhead general 'Black Tom Fairfax" at Langport and soundly beaten there also. He then marched to Exeter with what remained of his force and then further west in to the fanatically Royalist County of Cornwall to recruit new blood. He stayed there for several months basking in the glory of the title he had given himself, the 'General of the West'. After the final capitulation of the Royalist cause, and seemingly having lapsed in to alcoholism, he took a boat for France, but ended his days as an officer in Spain where he fully embraced the Catholic faith, some say for an inducement of money. The family estates that he left behind in England are now occupied by Buckingham Palace. He died in Madrid in 1657, aged forty-nine.

***

The Strangways:

Colonel James Strangways: The commander of the defeated Royalist garrison at Abbotsbury, having escaped to France after the siege, probably made his way back into England and the wars before the final fall of the King's cause. He died at a relatively young age in 1655.

***

Sir John Strangways: Outlived his younger son, James by eleven years, finally dying on the 30th December in that year of disaster 1666, aged a very creditable 82 years. After being taken prisoner at the siege of Sherborne Castle in 1645 he was held in the Tower of London and only released three years later. He is buried at the family's main seat at Melbury Sampford, to the north of Dorchester.

***

Colonel Giles Strangways:

The older brother, was captured with his father at Sherborne and likewise taken a prisoner to the Tower of London. He was only released after the family paid a fine of £10,000! The family was well connected and even had links with the Thynnes of Longleat House, the family of the present Lord Bath. In all, the Strangways' support for the Royalist cause cost them no less than £35,000, which in today's money is the equivalent of about £20,000.000. He became the MP for Bridport after the wars and died in 1675, also being buried at Melbury Sampford.

***

Sir Lewis Dyve:

By the August of 1645, Dyve was the Governor of Sherborne Castle and was being furiously besieged there by General (Black Tom) Fairfax. After a very stubborn and creditable defence, the castle fell, and Sir Lewis, his wife Howarda and her father and brothers, John and Giles Strangways were, with many others, taken prisoner and thrown in to the same jail at Poole that had previously contained Fabian Hodder only a few months before.

From there, Dyve was eventually transported to London and imprisoned in the Tower of London. The man who decided upon his choice of 'cellmate' could well have had a wonderfully wicked sense of humour, because the character that Dyve was destined to share his long captivity with could hardly have been more polarised in his views. Sir Lewis, the die-hard, archetypal Cavalier who could not even begin to comprehend that any man could ever take up arms against his King, was incarcerated with the Leveller leader, 'Freeborn' John Lilburn, a champion of the rights of the ordinary man.

The Levellers were Roundhead soldiers who 'agitated' within their regiments for better conditions and rights for their comrades. The movement became so strong that in 1647, it actually threatened the stability of the army, and Cromwell attacked a 5000 strong group of them at Burford in Oxfordshire as they slept in their various billets, eventually executing the ringleaders in the churchyard there after locking them up inside the church for three days without food or water, before they could link up with another Leveller group of similar numbers at Oxford. Had those two rebel forces managed to merge, England's history may well have been very different today.

Lilburn was an arch agitator, a political soldier and thinker, and was confined as a trouble-maker likely to disturb the peace. For a time he even enjoyed the admiration of no lesser figure than Oliver Cromwell, but was eventually broken by the fall of his Leveller cause and his long imprisonment both in the Tower and at Mount Orgueil in Jersey and died, some say, as a lunatic, in

Eltham in 1657, about two years after his final release. However, this great man, Lilburne, deserves to be remembered along with those other great English political freedom fighters and thinkers, such as Thomas Paine and George Loveless.

No one really knows what those two stalwarts of their own particular philosophies talked about during those long days and nights of incarceration alone in the Tower of London, but, their exchanges must have been absolutely priceless!

Dyve's jailer was John Lenthall, the elder brother of the speaker of the House of Commons and upon first meeting Sir Lewis, told him that he had *"heard him esteemed for a man of honour"* and that if Dyve would give him his word not to try to escape, then he would, *"esteem it the best security that could be given"*. The prisoner replied that Lenthall *"might be confident he would not break with him until first giving him fair warning"*.

Eventually a death sentence was passed on Dyve, but just hours before his appointment with the executioner on the 15th January 1648, he escaped in a very spectacular fashion.

Exactly how he managed to cheat death was the subject of an amusing passage from the pages of the celebrated Royalist diarist John Evelyn, who notes that on the 6th September 1651, Sir Lewis was among his guests for a dinner at St. Germain.

Evelyn wrote:

> *"He entertained us with his wonderful escape out of prison in Whitehall, the very evening he was to have been put to death, leaping down out of a 'Jakes' two storeys high into the Thames at high water, in the coldest of winter and at night, so as by swimming he got to a boat that attended for him, though he was guarded by six musketeers."*

To the delight of the assembled diners, Sir Lewis then apparently produced a flattened musket ball attached to several pieces of gold coin that were fused together and badly misshapen. He attributed their condition to the fact that they had been in his purse on the night of his escape and had saved his life by stopping the musket ball which was fired at him by his guards as he jumped from the window! No mean feat, for a man of 49, to jump forty or fifty feet in the middle of winter, in to the freezing River Thames at night.

Then again, what better incentive would one need than the sound of an axe being sharpened?

John Evelyn's closing observations of Dyve, this loyal, but sometimes unlucky soldier, may or may not have been a little harsh? He wrote: *"this knight was indeed a valiant gentleman… but, not a little given to romance when he spake of himself…"*

Dyve seems to have eventually made his way to Southern Ireland, as he is recorded as being one of the officers at the resounding defeat of the Royalist forces at the Battle of Rathmines and Baggorath near Dublin in August 1649. Also fighting here alongside him was Lord Inchiquin. Two thousand of Inchiquin men changed sides during the fighting.

Sir Lewis died on the 17th April 1669, aged 70 and is buried at Combhay in Somerset.

***

The Dorset Trained Bands

(with fighting units with surnames)

(Soldiers names and numbers all from the excellent transcriptions of Peachey & Turton's, The Fall of the West, 1994)

Sir Walter Erle was given the task of reviewing the Military forces of the County of Dorset in 1641 and found that there were two ill equipped troops of horse under Captains Thomas Hussey Esq and Angel Graye Esq.

There were nineteen companies of foot, of which at least thirteen are known about.

Companies	Musketeers	Pikemen
Phelips	88	68
Swayne	82	61
Fry	75	80
Ryves	83	71
Radford	88	46
Fitzjames	74	70
Freke	69	56
Hardy	67	65
Hussey	123	79
Hoskins	100?	80?
Larder	80	40
Sydenham	70	54
Goolde (Gould)	116	55

Towns	Musketeers	Pikemen
Dorchester and Puddletown	80?	75?
Lyme Regis	30	20
Weymouth	143	28
Melcombe	45	?
Isle of Portland	40	?
Isle of Purbeck	201	63
TOTAL	1,654	1,011

(111 un-armoured)

The Dorset Trained Bands marched north to fight the Scots in 1640, but the expedition was fraught with mutiny and dissent from the start. At Faringdon in Berkshire an officer named Lieutenant **Mohun** virtually severed his drummer's hand with a sword after they quarreled.

This so incensed his soldiers that they chased him and two other officers, a Captain **Lewknor** and an Ensign, into the upstairs of an inn. The three men were forced to flee out of a window and onto the swinging inn sign outside, where they tried to defend themselves with their swords. Lewknor and the Ensign jumped down and escaped, but Mohun was eventually dislodged with stones and fell heavily to the ground. The soldiers then seized him and *"smashed his brains out"* before throwing him in an open sewer. This still did not quite finish him though and upon seeing him attempt to get up, they then dragged him out and hung him upon a pillory where he finally succumbed to his injuries. Two men were eventually hanged for their part in the murder. Other officers on the ill-fated journey included **Troilus Turbeville** and **Bullen Reymes**.

Of the known 'trained bands units, few individual soldier's names are known, however many of them would probably have joined their officers' when they formed proper fighting units as the war began in earnest. One man that is known is Captain **Gould's** clerk, **John Daniell**.

Another Company which was either a trained band or possibly a Dorset volunteer unit was commanded by a Captain Churchill. This could possibly be the Royalist **William Churchill**, who was Deputy Governor of Dorchester and was captured by Francis Sydenham in December 1643.

*** = Christian name not known

The names of some of this unit are known:
Lieutenant **William Paty**, Ensign **William Whiteway** and Sergeant *** **Bale**

Common Soldiers: **Thomas Poole, John Bragge, Joseph Culfe, John Lobb, Richard Scobile, Samuell Bushros(e), William Lasilburie, Benjamin Gould, William Cleark, William Polden, Richard White, Joseph Underwood, Lidrid Baylie, Philip Suds, Thomas Coulsons, John Strong, Ellis Eursitt.**

***

Other similar units include Colonel **Thomas Trenchard**, Clerk *** **Prescott**, Captain *** **Broderip**, Captain *** **Floyer**, Sergeant **Peter Balston**, Clerk **Richard Stevens**.

Four companies that may have fought at the siege of Sherborne Castle in August and September 1642, or else were formed to supervise it destruction after it fell, were:

Captain **Humphrey Cory**, Clerk **James Cornish**, Captain **Gerrard Owen**, Carrier or Soldier **Charles Churchill**, Captain **William Lewis**, Lieutenant **Thomas Salmond**, Ensign **John Osbourne**, Captain **John Poyntz**, Sergeant *** **Ffoxwell**

Captain	Junior officers, NCOs and common soldiers
Henry Henlie	Not known
John Arthur	Not known
*** Harry	Not known
Henry Jarvis	Not known
Benjamin Bailie	Not known
*** Lacy	Not known
John Whiteway	Drummer **Joseph Michell**
Richard Savage	Lieutenant *** Terrie
*** Newdigate	Lieutenant *** **Taylor**, Cornet *** **Martin**, Quartermaster *** **Cheshire**, Corporal *** **Wilding**, Surgeon **John Jixure**
John Seward	Lieutenant **Edward Brag**, Ensign **Edward Dashwood**, Sergeants **Walter Huett** and **Nicholas Stone**, Drummers **Thomas Philips** and *** **Hilliard**
Joseph Paty	Lieutenant **Josiah Terry**, Ensign **John White**, Sergeants **Walter Huett** and **Nicholas Stone**, Drummer *** **Perrin**
Captain Lt. *** Smith	Ensign *** **Sinkleram**, Drummer **Morgan Moy**, Soldiers **Sam Carter**, **Robert Gillett**, **John Keale**, **William Keay**, **George Arnold**, **William Ashe**

There is mention of a few unidentified officers serving in the County: Captain **Guntir**, Captain **Baynard**, Captain **Symmes**, Lieutenant **Caylo**, Lieutenant **Danison**, Lieutenant **Janson**, Lieutenant **Janison**, Lieutenant **Napeese**.

The main garrison towns had their own Companies or Regiments to defend them at the outbreak of hostilities, or soon after. In fact, Melcombe had a trained militia as early as 9th July 1632, who were commanded by one **Henry**

Waltham, with **Owen Hollman** as Ensign and rather poignantly, a certain **John Cade** as Lieutenant who later became a leading Crabchurch Conspirator and was hanged for his involvement upon the Nothe gibbet thirteen years later.

Lyme Regis:

Lyme was under the protection of Colonel **Thomas Ceeley** and his regiment of foot. His immediate subordinates seem to have been Captain **Revet** and Lieutenant **Astwood.** Other officers present include Captains **William Davy, William Newell (Newhill?)** and **James Gache.**
Also Major **Refor Ceeley,** Lieutenant **Thomas Lou** and Ensign **William Browning.** Four sergeants were also mentioned, **John Hoodman, Thomas Fyrate, Richard Whytte** and **Daniell Gaccis** and, a man whose rank is not noted, **Cory Mollton.** Ordinary soldiers included **John James** and **Ben James** who were in **Captain Newhill**'s company and another common soldier **John Lester,** who was maimed.

Poole:

The main Captains were **John Howard** and **William Scutt.** There was also another Captain named **George Scutt** and an Ensign called **James Jewty.**

Dorchester:

Soldiers stationed in Dorchester at various times were fairly well documented. For example, a **Nicholas Cornew** and **Philip Cornew** of Taunton, also **William Hellett, John Hallett, (Hellett)** and **John Vincent** of Chardstock. **Josiah Bishop, William Morres, Moses Colfox, Henry Dunne, John Lovelase, William Parsons, John Holmead,** and **Thomas Sheppard,** a drummer, all of Bridport, **Thomas Chetnol** of Sherborne. **Christopher Maraker** and **Humphrey Staple** of Wambrooke. **Edward Craudon, Miles Priday, William Morris, William Munden** and **Hugh Munden** all of **Netherbury, William Wilson** 'stuff weaver' of Dorchester. **Edward Pitfold** of **Allington. John Grant** of **Loders. William Case** of **South Bowood. John Colborne** of Corfe Castle. **Nicholas Smith** of **Marshwood. Nathaniel White** of Osmington. **Richard Tawnton. Richard Morse** of Martinstowne, **Thomas Baily** of Hinton Martyn. **James Outen** of Wareham

In 1642, on the 1st of September, **Sir Walter Erle's** troop of horse consisted of 52 troopers. For about ten months one of them, **Theophilus Sacherevell** kept the accounts. Below are the names entered by the trooper with the grandiose name.

Officers/NCOs
Lieutenant *** **Johnson**, Quartermaster **Paul Schooley**, Cornet **Thomas Pyne**, Trumpeters **George Baily, Thomas Baywill**

Common Soldiers
Theophilus Sacherevell, Nicholas Bucks, John Popham, Viny Verrent, *** Mandon, *** Ploy, George Savage, James Gould, Andrew Joy, Roger Woodcock, Robert Bisshop, Thomas Sandford, Josip Lee, Thomas Seward, Mr James Vinery, William Ffloild, John Roberts, John Speedwing, Mr Alexander Langford, John Vincent, Hisrom Conway, Nathaniel Peacock, Josiah Tollonville, Mr Long, Gilbert Whitton, Josip Stroodley, Robert Williams, Mr Bragg, Mr Perrin, George Little, John Edwards, Henry Roenis, Roger Stivens, Robert Michill, Nicholas Chibbett, Henry Waltham, Andrew Middleson, Jos Wise, Mathiw Webber, Jos Roper, John Lee, Hin Elliot, Sam Huett, Richard Childe, William Coombes, Henry Daive, William Childe, William Portisson, Antony Coombes, George Hulett, Alex Toby, Thomas Young, Antony Vaskam, Jerome Conway, Henry Edwards.

By June 1643 the personnel of Erle's troop had changed considerably:

Officers/NCOs
Lieutenant Captain *** **Johnson**, Cornet *** **Williams**, Quartermaster *** **Johnson**, Corporals *** **Brocker**, *** **Squibb** and **Francis Peek**, Trumpeters **Gregory Baylie** and **Hugh Cooke**

Common Soldiers
Robert Collins, Thomas Kickwell, William Cobias, John Valimer, Giles Marsh, John Smith, John Grant, John Hutten, George Oliver, Antigonie Ingram, John Maurice, Richard Kitts, William Haytd, Nicholas Crimble, John Harris, Richard Gird, Lawrence Wick, Joseph See, Edward Webber, George Primrose, William Kitts, Henry Huett, Edward Calwind, John Staple, Michael Hardinge, Lawrence Devinish, Henry Staple, Thomas Chatnell, Robert Lambert, Nicholas Cobie, Josiah Dewry, M Younger, Mr Bennet, Mr Port, Walter Horfford, (Horsford?) , Richard Lymbic, William Attwood, Mark Perkins, Thomas Perrin, Mr Russell, Will Fford, Mr Paine, John Stocker, Michael Dewty, William Hallet, Roger Stevens, John Cleve, Valentine Paull, George Hulett, Antigone Combes, Mr Symbingbourne, Alexander Tobie, Phillip Mells, Anthonie Vincent, William Watts, Mr Bossr, Jermiah Conway, Arthur Long, *** Hanrie, Theophilus Sacherevell, Robert Smith, Julius Paine, Antonie Jennett, William Humingbourne, John Short

On the 8th of April 1647, the regimental accountant **Theophilus Sacherevell** put in a petition along with his comrade, **William Childe** and 35 other soldiers complaining that they were owed 15 weeks arrears of pay to the value of £13/2s/6d whilst serving under **Sir Walter Erle.**

Erle also had a troop of Dragoons (mounted infantry) and the known members of this unit were as follows:

Robert Sevule, Robert Waller, John Sprayne, Toby Ffany, Edmund Collier, Thomas Ritshiz (Riches?), John Wormhill, Stephen Slibbs, William Hallett, Joseph Hill, George Ffitshott, Antony Smith, James Bazily, Oliver Fox, Roger Strodly, John Colbourn, Edward Mitchell, James Outing & Richard Pittman of Bere Regis, **Edward Lunt, George Giles,** *** **Craylea**

***

Erle's Dragoons seem to have been a short-lived unit, as by mid 1643 only **Francis Sydenham**'s Dragoons are operational for the Parliamentary side in Dorset. These were an effective, tough unit with many successes to their name, and were a credit to their leader. Those soldiers known were as follows:

Officers/NCOs
Captain **Francis Sydenham**, Lieutenant *** **Vabason**, Cornet **Edward Masters**, Quartermaster **George Sydenham**, Scoutmaster (?) **Robert Wise**, Sergeant **Daniel Seward**, Drummer *** **Pouncey**

Common Soldiers
George Wise (servant to Cornet Masters?) **Thomas Wilkinson, Will Ffintoffie, John Sawkins, Will Michill, Philip Clemints, Samuel Cooper, John Coltman, Will King, Thomas Eaves, M Smith, Henry Taylor, William Smith, Sam Baker, Christopher Young, Edward Cox, John Holswort, John Bishop**

***

William Sydenham's initial troop of horse, formed in **April 1643** is less well documented as far as personnel are concerned. Those that are recorded were:-

Officers/NCOs
Captain **William Sydenham**, Lieutenant **George Snellinge**, Cornet *** **Tiree**, Quartermaster *** **Barnet**, Corporals **Henry Ford** and *** **Tillie**

<u>Common Soldiers</u>
Robert Farnam, James Moore, Abraham Baltimore, Samuel Swaffield, Thomas Parsons.

***

The Staff in Dorset, headed by **Erle** at the start of the war included as Chief Surgeon and Apothecary, **Peter de Salanova** and his assistant **John Jixure** (?)

The Provost Marshall was **Mr Peter White.**

The Chief Scoutmaster was **Thomas Clench** and his assistant was **John Bushwood.**

The Wagon Master was **Richard Windsor.**

The Quartermaster General was **Henry Bridges.**

The Commissary for Victuals was **Richard Williams.**

References

Bayley, A.R. (1910) *Great Civil War in Dorset.* Taunton

Brady, G. (2012) *The Great Rejection of 1662.* Evangelical Press

Clarendon, The Earl of, E. Hyde, (1807) *History of the Rebellion and Civil Wars in England.* Clarendon Press

Cowdell-Barrett, W.E. (1910) *The Surprise of the Forts of Weymouth.* (Copied by Rev. Cowdell-Barrett, February 1910)

Dewhurst, K (1966) *Doctor Thomas Sydenham* University of California Press

Eve, J (2006) *The Diaries of John Evelyn.* Everyman

Hutchins, J (1861). *The History & Antiquities of Dorset.* J.B. Nichols

Payne, J.F (1900) *Masters of Medicine.* Longmans, Green & Co, New York

Peachey, S & Turton, A. (1994) *War in the West: The Fall of the West Pt.1 (English Civil War Battles) (Vol 4).*Stuart Press

Ricketts, E. (1979) *The Buildings of Old Weymouth.* Longman's

Sydenham, G.F. (1928) *History of the Sydenham Family.* E. Dwelly, Surrey

Sydenham, J. (1839) *The History of the Town and London.* Whittaker & Co

Underdown, D. (1853) *Fire from Heaven.* Yale University Press; paperbound Ed edition (Dec 1994) Whitlocke's Memorials University Press (1853)

Williams, S (2012) *The Treasure of the Golden Grape.* Deadman's Bay Publishing

Acknowledgements

Much thanks to…

Katie Brown-Gurley, for presenting me with the original 'Sydenham letter' at no small expense to herself.

Debby Rose, author, without whose help, energy and expertise, this book would not originally have been attempted.

Matilda Vine for her excellent proof-reading skills, superb technical know-how and very good advice.

Semirani Vine for her excellent artistry and friendship, and Morwenna Vine for her support and great cups of tea.

Marloes Visser, for resurrecting the original manuscript for me to work on.

Julie Freeman, for providing me with copies of the Peter Ince diary and witness statements.

Selwyn Williams, author, for all his help, knowledge and good guidance.

Corfe Castle photograph Jill Walker
Photograph of author with Ronald Hutton by Mark North (Dark Dorset)
Sandsfoot Castle photograph by Marloes Visser
Photographs from Abbotsbury by Steve Booth

All other photographs by Mark Vine

Illustrations, maps and front cover by Semirani Vine

In 2009, internationally renowned Celtic Folk Rock band, The Dolmen, released an album based upon the events highlighted in this book and the English Civil War in general, called The Crabchurch Conspiracy'.
The music was written by band members Taloch Jameson and Josh Elliott, with the lyrics being written by Mark Vine.

The album can be sampled and purchased at
www.thedolmen.com